My friend Kevin Harvey has given us a creative, lighthearted, and precise perspective of the Bible in pop culture. Pop culture doesn't often get the Bible right, but make no mistake about it, pop culture, regardless of motive, does get Bible. If current trends are any indication, we can expect more Bible, not less.

—Steve Wright, disciple pastor, First Baptist Church West Palm Beach

Kevin Harvey's new book *All You Want to Know about the Bible in Pop Culture* is a powerful reminder that God shows up in the most unexpected places. The Bible itself may not be front-page news today, but its indelible imprint on our culture continues.

—Phil Cooke, filmmaker, media consultant, and author of
Unique: Telling Your Story in the Age of Brands and Social Media

My friend Kevin demonstrates cultural awareness and biblical devotion in this insightful and enjoyable book. As one who often uses music and films to illustrate my sermon points, *All You Want to Know about the Bible in Pop Culture* gave me several new ideas. He made me aware of numerous spiritual parallels in pop culture. I recommend it to anyone who is seeking to communicate biblical truth to a media-literate world and to anyone searching for truth, meaning, and eternal beauty—and that's all of us.

—Tony Merida, founding pastor, Imago Dei Church, Raleigh, NC

ALL YOU WANT TO KNOW ABOUT

THE BIBLE IN POP Culture

FINDING OUR CREATOR
IN SUPERHEROES, PRINCE CHARMING, AND OTHER MODERN MARVELS

KEVIN HARVEY

THOMAS NELSON
Since 1798

NASHVILLE   MEXICO CITY   RIO DE JANEIRO

Published in Nashville, Tennessee, by Thomas Nelson. Thomas Nelson is a trademark of HarperCollins Christian Publishing, Inc.

Thomas Nelson titles may be purchased in bulk for educational, business, fund-raising, or sales promotional use. For information, please e-mail SpecialMarkets@ThomasNelson.com.

Page design and layout: Crosslin Creative
Images: www.dollarphotoclub.com, dreamstime.com, istock.com

Bible Brain Builders taken from *Bible Brain Builders Vol. 1* and *Bible Brain Builders Vol. 2*, © 2011 by Thomas Nelson. The material in this section originally was published in other forms in *Nelson's Super Book of Bible Word Games, Book 1*, © 1992, *Nelson's Super Book of Bible Word Games, Book 2*, © 1993, *Nelson's Super Book of Bible Word Games, Book 3*, © 1993, *Incredible Mazes, Book 1*, © 1993, *Incredible Mazes, Book 2*, © 1994, *Nelson's Amazing Bible Trivia Book 2* © 2000, 2011 by Thomas Nelson. All rights reserved.

Unless otherwise noted, Scripture quotations in the Brain Builders section are taken from THE NEW KING JAMES VERSION. © 1982 by Thomas Nelson, Inc. Used by permission. All rights reserved.

Verses marked KJV are taken from the HOLY BIBLE: KING JAMES VERSION.

Unless otherwise indicated, Scripture quotations are taken from *The Voice*™ *translation*. © 2012 Ecclesia Bible Society. Used by permission. All rights reserved.*

* Note: Italics in quotations from *The Voice* are used to "indicate words not directly tied to the dynamic translation of the original language" but that "bring out the nuance of the original, assist in completing ideas, and . . . provide readers with information that would have been obvious to the original audience" (*The Voice*, preface). Emphasis in quotations from *The Voice* is indicated with the use of **boldface** type.

Scripture quotations marked (NIV) are taken from the Holy Bible, New International Version®, NIV®. Copyright © 1973, 1978, 1984, 2011 by Biblica, Inc.™ Used by permission of Zondervan. All rights reserved worldwide. www.zondervan.com The "NIV" and "New International Version" are trademarks registered in the United States Patent and Trademark Office by Biblica, Inc.™

Scripture quotations marked (NLT) are taken from the Holy Bible, New Living Translation, copyright © 1996, 2004, 2007, 2013 by Tyndale House Foundation. Used by permission of Tyndale House Publishers, Inc., Carol Stream, Illinois 60188. All rights reserved.

ISBN: 978-0-7180-0551-1

Printed in the United States of America

15 16 17 18 19 20 [RRD] 6 5 4 3 2 1

To Amy.
How could this be for anyone else but the one who
has believed in and supported me all this time?

CONTENTS

INTRODUCTION
The Art of Our Time

Can you keep a secret?

You better lean in close; we don't want the powers that be in the entertainment industry to hear this. And don't start any hashtags either. If the E! Network notices this trending, we could disturb the little baby sleeping peacefully on the corner of Hollywood Boulevard and Broadway. Let's just keep this to ourselves, okay?

All right, here it is. . . .

Pop culture loves the Bible.

Now zip it. Quietly turn around and go back to watching your animated movies that speak to your identity in Jesus. Return to your couch and your Keurig and enjoy the next marathon of your favorite reality show depicting a family not unlike those we find in the Bible. And carefully slip on your headphones and (not too loud!) jam to your favorite MTV artist talking to God. Let's act normal, people. There's nothing to see here. . . .

Okay, so we're clearly joking. There's no need to keep this secret. Scream it from the middle of Best Buy. Get on your iPhone and hashtag away. (#BibleInPopCulture, #HollywoodAndBible, #BieberLovesBible, to get you started.) And the truth is, I'm not even sure how much of a secret it really is. After all, why would pop culture, and the entertainment industry specifically, not love the Bible? Inside this best-selling book, we read stories of little shepherd-boy David versus the behemoth Goliath, a disciple betraying his friend and then hanging himself out of remorse, people beaten up and left for dead being nursed back to health by the unlikeliest of passersby, epic battles of three hundred versus tens of thousands, horrific moments of bloodshed, and an apocalyptic ending too frightening for even the big screen.

Inside the Bible, we also find the ultimate love story, the highest of sacrifices, the fulfillment of purpose, unimaginable grace for even the most lost of souls, and redemption found for all mankind. It's the feel-good story of every year.

And the popularity of the Bible in pop culture goes well beyond the more obvious biblical stories to have found success on both the big and small screens. But these certainly don't hurt the argument being made here. Take these R-rated movies, for example: *The Hangover* (all three of them), *Ted*, *Saving Private Ryan*, *300*, *21 Jump Street*. The most successful of those (*The Hangover*) still came up over $90 million short of the $370 million that Mel Gibson's *The Passion of the Christ* brought in back in 2004 when it became (and remains as of this writing) the all-time box office champion for an R-rated movie.[1]

Almost a decade later, in the spring of 2013, the History Channel and über-producer Mark Burnett (of *Survivor* and *The Apprentice* fame) released *The Bible*, a ten-hour miniseries based on stories taken straight from . . . well, the Bible. The first episode premiered to an audience of 13.1 million people, and over the next ten weeks maintained that number with an average of 13.19 million total viewers, making it the third-most-watched cable show of all of 2013—almost 5 million more viewers than the mega-hit *Breaking Bad*.[2]

The same people who brought us *The Bible* followed it up in February 2014 with a movie adaptation called *Son of God* that brought in more than $25 million its opening weekend, higher than the opening weekend box office of most other major releases that same month, including: *The Monuments Men*, *Three Days to Kill*, *Pompeii*, *RoboCop*, *Endless Love*, and *Winter's Tale*—most with bigger budgets and more popular actors attached to their vehicles. And in December 2013 NBC announced that it was signing Burnett to produce a follow-up series to *The Bible* based on the book of Acts, expected to be released in the spring of 2015.

Mel Gibson and Mark Burnett aren't the only ones filling the entertainment industry with the Bible, however. Usually it's much more subtle and sometimes without even its creator's intent to do so. But God, the sovereign Creator, will always find a way to reach his creations. And he's not afraid to use pop culture to do so.

★ ★ ★

Picture in your mind different eras of culture as being represented as one big pyramid much like one built by Pharaoh and the Egyptians. Imagine on top of this pyramid that represents culture an insanely huge block of ice, way too big to even really balance on top of a pyramid. (But we're just imagining, so it's okay.) This massive block of ice represents the Bible, and the very top of the pyramid on which it balances represents the era around the early Middle Ages when the biblical canon was finalized and the Bible basically became the culture.

The lower you go down on the pyramid, the more recent periods it represents, past the Middle Ages, through the Victorian era, the Industrial Revolution, and into the twenty-first century. As that block of ice (representing the Bible) melts, of course it's going to flow through and cover more of the skinnier areas of the pyramid at its zenith. In the Middle Ages, the Bible and religion was the culture and what most of the laws, traditions, and opinions were built around. When trade and literacy began evolving more quickly at the end of the Middle Ages, due in part to the invention of the printing press, the Bible became more widely available to the people than it had ever been before, and they began reading and studying it more independently and interpreting it without clerical assistance. However, they also began reading Shakespeare, Cervantes, and Montaigne. The philosophical ideas of Francis Bacon, who "proposed a pursuit of knowledge that stood apart from faith, rather than blended with faith,"[3] as well as those of many other scholars and philosophers, began spreading. Suddenly, the Bible was no longer *the* book, but one among many.

But still, the ice kept melting and slowly creeping down the pyramid. It certainly did not cover as much as it did at the top, but its downward flow could not be stopped. Even today, as wide as that pyramid is, the ice keeps melting and seeping through the cracks, weaving its way down the cultural pyramid. As cable channels multiply, new movie studios pop up, more and more books hit the Kindle shelves, and celebrities are made on YouTube, there's a great deal more of the pyramid to cover, and yet the water continues to find its way through more of it than one may realize. You only need to know what to look for.

From LEGOs to *Lost*, Miley to *The Mindy Project*, Superman to Sheldon Cooper, and a great deal more, today's pop culture is still allowing the thirst-quenching Bible to seep its way into the cracks of its foundation. Clearly, culture still finds the Bible extremely relevant, even if some don't even recognize how God's Word has helped shaped their art. Pop culture has begun the dialogue; will the church continue it?

* * *

In the sixth century BC, King Nebuchadnezzar of Babylon invaded Judah and forced the surviving Israelites into exile. In the early years of this exile, Nebuchadnezzar ordered one of his chiefs to educate some of the young Israelites in the "language and literature of the Chaldeans, *the people who lived in Babylonia*" (Dan. 1:4). He wanted "fit young men with no *physical or moral* infirmities, handsome, skilled in all wisdom, knowledgeable, discerning, and understanding" (v. 4). Four of the young men chosen were Daniel, Hananiah, Mishael, and Azariah. (The latter three would come to be known more famously as Shadrach, Meshach, and Abed-nego.)

The Bible says that after three years God had given these four "an unusual aptitude for learning the literature and science of the time" (v. 17 NLT 1996). Nebuchadnezzar was so impressed with these four that he appointed them to his regular staff of advisors and found the advice of these young men to be "ten times better than that of all the magicians and enchanters in his entire kingdom" (v. 20 NLT 1996). Two more kings would succeed Nebuchadnezzar, which led to a fiery furnace, a lions' den, and finally this proclamation from King Darius: "I decree that all people everywhere who live under my sovereign rule ought to tremble before and fear the God of Daniel. For He is the living God, and He will endure forever" (Dan. 6:26).

The king of the very civilization that had taken the Israelites into exile acknowledged that the God of Israel is *the* God. All this as a result of four teenagers whom God gave "an unusual aptitude for learning the literature and science of the time."

Like those four heroes of the Bible, would you dare to join me in learning more of the art of our time and see what God can do through us?

CHAPTER 1

MAYBE *the* S

Stands
for
SAVIOR

They flood our movie theaters every summer and our streets every Halloween. They fill the shelves of comic book stores and the hallways of Comic-Con. Some can fly and catch bullets with their teeth; others are mere mortals with cool gadgets. Some consider their alter ego a curse, while others see it as their calling.

Whatever the case, whoever the superhero, the world is fascinated with them. Considering that almost eighty years after Superman's comic book debut in 1938, movie audiences will be lining up to see him in a (please, please, pleeeaaase be) legendary movie that also stars Batman and Wonder Woman, it's safe to say the extreme popularity of superheroes is not just a fad trending online for a few days. And perhaps there is something to say about that. Maybe our fascination with superheroes is because we are being drawn to something innate in us. A longing for something more. Something perfect. Something supernatural.

At some point in their lives, most people look in the mirror and see their deep flaws. They realize their physical limits, that they are not as invincible as they thought they once were. They have come to terms that they are not

Is it possible that Superman, the world's first comic book superhero, was inspired, intentionally or not, by the only real Superhero?

capable of rescuing themselves out of every hole they fall into. And they know they need help.

And a few of these flawed, limited humans created superheroes for the world to enjoy. People who were capable of doing what we couldn't. But is it possible that Superman, the world's first comic book superhero, was inspired, intentionally or not, by the only real Superhero? Take this verse, for example: "Even though you've been raised as a human being, you are not one of them. They could be a great people . . . if they wish to be. They only lack the light to show the way. For this reason above all, their capacity for good, I have sent them you, my only son"[1] (1 Superman 3:1).

Did I have you there for a minute? This sounds like something God might've told Jesus as he was being baptized, right? It's at least more biblical than some of what others seem to think is in the Bible, such as the faux verse "God helps those who helps themselves."

Jesus was raised as a human being, although he wasn't exactly like the rest of them. Check.

Jesus told us he is the light of the world. Check.

Jesus is God's only Son. Check.

It turns out Superman had a few things in common with Jesus. The previous quote is taken straight from the 2006 film *Superman Returns*. It was even chosen as the narration for the film's preview that was released the previous year. And to top it all off, the actual line delivered by actor Marlon Brando was taken from cut footage of the original 1978 *Superman*.

Superman may have been the first superhero (at least the first one with supernatural abilities) given to us in 1938, but there has been no shortage of new ones given to us since. Beginning with what is known as the Golden Age of comic books (c. 1938–1950) when we were given Superman, Batman, Green Lantern, and Captain America, among others, to the Silver Age (c. 1956–1970) that brought us Iron Man, the Fantastic Four, Hulk, Spider-Man, and more, we could write pages upon pages listing the superheroes in the Marvel and DC Comics universes alone.

In the dates of these two comic book eras, as well as the recent boom of superhero movies in the last decade-plus, there is one undeniable common theme that perhaps sheds some light on the culture's sudden need for such supernatural heroes in their lives.

War.

The Golden Age paralleled World War II and the unrest the world felt with the rise of Hitler's Third Reich. When the war ended, so did the popularity of many comics; but the Silver Age emerged when conflict rose again, this time in Vietnam, as well as the nuclear arms chess match of the Cold War. And between this writing and when the War on Terror began in late 2001, we have had six X-Men movies, five Spider-Mans, three Batmans, three Iron-Mans, two Supermans, two Hulks, two Thors, two Captain Americas, and one too many Green Lantern movies.

When war surrounds us and evil rears its ugly head, we look for good to prevail. When soldiers are dying to defend freedoms, we search to find a higher purpose emerging from their sacrifices. Many find comfort in God our Creator

NOTE TO COMIC BOOK *Loyalists* Who Are about to Put Me on THEIR BLACKLIST

This chapter on superheroes is based entirely on recent movie adaptations, not on any of the comic series that have been around for decades. Although I'm sure a much more involved literary piece would result from a study based on the thousands of comic books written on these four characters, I have chosen to write a condensed chapter based only on a handful of movies. Perhaps my brother, who if his house was on fire would carry out his wife in one arm and his comic books in the other, could one day write that book.

and the Bible, his message to us. Others perhaps resist this dependence on God but still seek supernatural comfort in heroes created during times of crisis.

If we could see God in Superman, the first superhero, it would stand to reason that we could also find him in many of the others inspired by Superman. After all, to mimic something is to pay the greatest compliment to it. Although no movie or comic book could ever get away with mixing DC and Marvel Comics superheroes, the following is one geek's version of a different type of Avengers. Four superheroes whose recent Hollywood depictions together paint a vivid picture of the true Superhero.

NOTE TO MY PASTOR *Friends* Who Are about to Put Me on THEIR BLACKLIST

Don't worry, my brethren. I believe Captain America said it best in *The Avengers* when warned about the dangers of going after the gods Thor and Loki: "There's only one God, ma'am, and I'm pretty sure he doesn't dress like that."[2]

⬇ SUPERMAN: THE HOPE FOR ALL MANKIND

It turns out the previews for *Superman Returns* were the best things about the movie. After a disappointed fan base showed little interest in seeing what would happen next for the original superhero, the studio's plans for sequels were scrapped, and they returned to the drawing board. But in the summer of 2013, *Man of Steel* put Superman back on fans' radars in a big way. In fact, before summer's end, plans for the sequel had already begun.

But even when a new director took a completely different direction with the Superman franchise, the resulting film was still filled with Christ comparisons. There are minor things to take notice of, such as a young Clark Kent

WHERE THE *Similarities* END . . .

While Clark emulated Jesus quite well when he opted to turn the other cheek to the diner who poured a pitcher of beer over him, I'm not quite sure Jesus would've later picked up the man's semi-truck and punctured it with a tree.

reading the philosophies of Plato, just as a young Jesus certainly read and studied the Torah. Clark is also thirty-three years old at the climax of the film, the age many scholars believe Jesus to have been at the time of his death.

An adolescent Clark Kent also watches his earthly father, Jonathan Kent, die in a tornado, something he could have prevented had his father felt the world was ready to see what his son could do. Compare this with Jesus at the wedding in Cana when a miracle is asked of him, yet he responded, "My time has not arrived" (John 2:4).

While he was alive, though, Jonathan Kent struggled with his fear that the world wouldn't understand his son. "When the world finds out what you can do, it's gonna change everything," Jonathan shares with his young son. "Our beliefs, our notions of what it means to be human. Everything. . . . People are afraid of what they don't understand."[3]

Surely Joseph had similar struggles concerning Jesus, the boy he raised as his own son. When Mary became pregnant with a child who was not his, Joseph had in mind to divorce her quietly until an angel told him who the baby was. We can only speculate Joseph's reactions, but protecting Jesus became uppermost in his mind, as indicated by their mad dash to Egypt in order to flee the wrath of Herod. For no longer was his priority to protect young Mary from public disgrace; rather, he found himself suddenly responsible for helping to protect and raise a child who would save the people from their sins. This child was the hope that a world crying out to God had been waiting for.

It is in this theme of hope that we find the heart of *Man of Steel*. Upon meeting his biological father for the first time, Clark (whose Kryptonian name, he learns, is Kal-El) is told, "The symbol of the house of El means hope."[4] And this is the symbol placed on his chest that resembles an *S*. His father, Jor-El, sent his only son to Earth to bring the people hope.

The hope that God sent to earth was his Son, Jesus. From Adam and Eve in the garden, to the Israelites wandering in the desert, to the people of Israel who had been conquered by foreign kingdoms, the Old Testament is filled with people calling out for help. They desperately needed God's intervention. They knew they were broken, sinful, and without hope on their own. In response, God "gave His only Son so that whoever believes in Him will not face everlasting destruction, but will have everlasting life" (John 3:16).

Though the world's need for everlasting hope was fulfilled two thousand years ago when Jesus came to earth, it has by no means been realized by all. We oftentimes find ourselves fighting our need for hope. It does not make

IF *Jesus* WERE A SUPERHERO . . .

▶ **He'd be of miraculous origins.**

"A virgin will conceive and bear a Son." (Matt. 1:23)

▶ **He'd wait to reveal himself.**

"Dear woman . . . My time has not arrived." (John 2:4)

▶ **He'd walk through walls.**

"The doors were locked; but suddenly, as before, Jesus was standing among them." (John 20:26 NLT)

▶ **He'd be able to disguise himself.**

"Jesus catches up to them and begins walking with them, but for some reason they don't recognize Him." (Luke 24:15–16)

sense that we need someone not of this world to save us. Nor do we understand why a father would love a people so much he would send his only son to die for them. And the confusion makes us afraid. Afraid of our vulnerability, of our fragility, of our dependency.

The people of Metropolis certainly did not immediately realize their need for Superman when General Zod tried to create a new planet of Krypton out of the foundation of earth, which would have resulted in billions of deaths; but that didn't change the fact that they did, indeed, desperately need him. And countless millions today also trudge through their days crying out for hope, not knowing that it has already come.

SPIDER-MAN: WHO THE WORLD NEEDS

In the middle act of the 2004 film *Spider-Man 2*, Peter Parker is having identity issues. "Am I not supposed to have what I want? What I need?" he asks himself. "What am I supposed to do?"[5] For Peter, his desire to live a normal life and the people's need for Spider-Man has brought him to a crossroads. He has been breaking promises to friends, missing classes, and having trouble keeping jobs because of his twenty-four-hour on-call job as the hero of New York City.

WHERE THE *Similarities* END . . .

As Jesus showed when he ascended to heaven after his resurrection, he knows how to end on a high note. He would've never made *Spider-Man 3*.

After taking a tumble in an alley one night, Peter takes off his Spider-Man outfit and drops it in a Dumpster, declaring to himself that he will be . . .
Spider-Man no more.

> **What if, on that fateful night in the garden, Jesus had stood up, seeing Judas and his eventual arrestors in the far-off distance, and declared that he would be . . . God no more?**

Like Peter, Jesus, too, was a man (but of the, you know, actually lived variety). At times he was hungry, tempted, and tired. He cut up with his friends, shared inside jokes with his family, and got blisters on his hands after a hard day's work. And while praying in the Garden of Gethsemane the night before his crucifixion, he is said to have been in so much agony that his sweat was like drops of blood. What if, on that fateful night in the garden, he had stood up, seeing Judas and his eventual arrestors in the far-off distance, and declared that he would be . . .

God no more?

No arrest. No trial. No scourging. No crucifixion. Who could blame him for leaving all that behind?

However . . .

That would have also meant no resurrection. No Savior. No Redeemer. No hope.

Just like Peter's decision to simply be a good kid living a normal life meant no more hero of New York City, especially for his neighbor Henry. As Aunt May told Peter, "Kids like Henry need a hero—courageous, self-sacrificing people, setting examples for all of us. Everybody loves a hero. People line up for them, cheer them, scream their names, and years later they'll tell how they stood in the rain for hours just to get a glimpse of the one who told them to hold on longer. . . . He [Henry] needs him [Spider-Man]."[6] Henry needed a self-sacrificing hero, and thankfully for New York City, Peter realized that before it was too late.

After Peter chooses to be Spider-Man again, there is a pivotal, climactic scene in which he takes off his mask and uses all his strength to stop an out-of-control train full of passengers from crashing off the end of the tracks, nearly losing his life in the process. When the train finally stops, Peter collapses into the passengers' arms, unmasked, as they carefully carry him, arms out at his sides in a cross position, over their heads. He showed them he was both hero and man as he willingly offered up his life for theirs.

Hebrews 2:14 explains why it was so important for Jesus to become human flesh for us: "Because God's children are human beings—made of flesh and blood—the Son also became flesh and blood" (NLT). However, having Jesus as simply a good flesh-and-blood teacher living a moral life wouldn't have helped us. We needed him on that cross. We needed him to choose to give up his life for us, for only "he could offer a sacrifice that would take away the sins of the people" (v. 17 NLT).

Jesus chose to be both man and God for our sakes. And had he not willingly done so, the consequences for us would've been a lot worse than a train derailment or an increase in crime. Without him as fully both, the world would not have the Savior it so desperately needs: the one who can both forgive us of our sins and substitute himself in place of the punishment we deserve.

BATMAN: NOT A HERO, BUT SOMETHING MORE

In the final scene of the blockbuster film *The Dark Knight*, Batman willingly takes the blame for murders he did not commit so that the legacy of Gotham's prized district attorney—the one who actually committed the murders—would not be tarnished. He is forced to go into hiding while the city and Gotham

WHERE THE *Similarities* END . . .

I can't imagine the crowd listening to Jesus' Sermon on the Mount would've heard much of what he had to say had he tried speaking with Batman's scary, raspy, prank-phone-call-making voice.

"What did you say? Blessed are the who? Stop talking like that. You're scaring my daughter!"

police accuse him of crimes he did not commit. As he runs into the night to avoid the police dogs tracking him, one boy who knows the truth asks his dad, "Why is he running, Dad? . . . He didn't do anything wrong."[7]

Batman had never been concerned with how the law viewed him. Despite many on the police force not agreeing with how he did things to help the people of Gotham, he always knew he had the people's best interests in mind and could not be deterred. He was never interested in taking credit; his only motivation was what he told the villain Ra's Al Ghul: "Gotham isn't beyond saving."[8]

When the Joker threatened to begin killing someone every hour until Batman revealed himself, the Gotham citizens who had always loved Batman quickly turned on him too. Suddenly Batman had neither the law on his side nor a cheering crowd in his corner.

But Batman was never about making friends either, only about saving the people of Gotham, no matter what they thought of him. As his longtime guardian Alfred told him, "Even if everyone hates [Batman] for it, that's the sacrifice he's making. . . . He's not being a hero; he's being something more."[9] And "something more" would soon mean, for the sake of the city he loved, willingly taking the blame for murders committed by a crazed district attorney who had tried killing him.

I don't know of anyone who can relate to the sacrifice Batman made.

Except maybe for one.

The Dark Knight trilogy is not a feel-good superhero story at all. But neither is the picture it replicates of how an innocent Jesus, with law and crowd turned against him, willingly took the punishment for sins he did not commit, all for the sake of the people he loved. Even Jesus' executioner, Pilate, knew he was innocent of the crimes he was being accused of (Matt. 27:11–26), yet Jesus refused to fight the injustice being thrown his way, for as Ephesians 5:2 says, "Christ loved us and gave himself up for us as a fragrant offering and sacrifice to God" (NIV).

I don't know of anyone who can relate to the sacrifice Batman made. Except maybe for one.

Why would Jesus do such a thing? Why did Batman? Perhaps Alfred said it best: "He [Batman] can make the choice that no one else can make—the right choice."[10]

Batman made the right choice for the people of Gotham by allowing them to believe he committed these crimes. Without his sacrifice, the people of Gotham would have lost hope.

Jesus made the right choice for you and me by giving himself up to be crucified. Without his sacrifice, the people of the world would have no hope.

The Dark Knight trilogy is tough to watch at times. It has a realism to it that, more than any other superhero film, hits home for us in the post-9/11 world. The violence can be excessive and uncomfortable. But even more uncomfortable is watching a once cheered-upon hero becoming something more—"a sacrifice of atonement" (Rom. 3:25 NIV).

WHERE'S THE SUPERHERO/SAVIOR CHAPTER ON . . .

Daredevil?—Sorry. He has horns on his head.

Ghost Rider?—Really? Am I the only one here who draws the line at making a deal with the devil?

Iron Man?—Rule of thumb: If someone's ego resembles King Saul's, they're definitely not looking like the Son of God.

Wolverine?—You have to smile every now and then if you want to remind people of Jesus.

THOR: THE DEATH AND RESURRECTION OF A KING

Stop me if this sounds familiar: The son of a great deity is sent to earth to live as a man. While many are skeptical of who he is, a few have chosen to believe. When the enemy comes after him, he sacrifices himself for the sake of the people on earth. And just when the enemy believes he has won and finally conquered the mighty son, our hero is risen from the dead, more powerful than ever, and showing all the world once and for all who he truly is . . . Jesus the Messiah—uh, sorry, got ahead of myself—Thor, long golden-haired, buff-beyond-imagination Norse god of thunder.

Thor's origin goes well beyond a comic book. Before he was the gentleman courting Natalie Portman on the big screen, before Marvel Comics legend Stan Lee introduced him to the comic world in 1962, Thor was a red-headed god in Norse mythology who rode in a chariot pulled by two goats, fought a serpent with his hammer, and fathered children with multiple goddesses.

I just lost some of you, didn't I? Was it the red-headed part?

WHERE THE *Similarities* END . . .

Jesus used a hammer to build furniture, not kill Frost Giants.

But as I have already said, I'm not concerned with the comic story of our superheroes. And in Thor's case, I'm definitely not looking at the real (but fake) god of Scandinavian lore. No, I'm more interested in director Kenneth Branagh's 2011 big-screen interpretation of our hero, specifically his death and resurrection scene in the final act.

Thor had been living on earth as a mortal, after having been banished there by his father for his reckless behavior. This noteworthy scene begins when his brother, Loki, sends to earth a great weapon called the Destroyer in order to kill Thor and anyone else around him.

In a small NEW MEXICO town, Thor—a god living as man—walks slowly up a dusty street toward the Destroyer, which is breathing large gulfs of fire at everything in its way. Bystanders run for cover all around.[11]

As Thor approaches his imminent death, he tells his brother listening from Asgard to leave the people around him alone. "Take mine and end this," he pleads.

The Destroyer steps back momentarily before taking a deadly swat at Thor, causing him to fly back about fifty feet. Jane runs to a dying Thor, who lies there struggling to breathe. "It's over," he tells her with his last bit of strength, before finally breathing out his last breath.

Far away in Asgard, Thor's father sheds a tear over the sacrifice of his son. Then Thor's hammer, which has been stuck in the ground fifty miles away, suddenly flies out of the ground at lightning speed straight for Thor, who miraculously sticks his hand up to catch the hammer just as it approaches him. Thor, suddenly alive and well, is immediately clothed in armor and royalty as he turns toward the Destroyer.

Jane stands there in awe, struggling for the right words to say. All she can manage is, "Oh . . . my . . . God."

The weather surrounding the immediate area grows dark. Wind, thunder, and lightning surround as Thor battles the Destroyer, leading quickly to its destruction.

Let's see this scene again, this time with some comparisons to Jesus' death and resurrection:

In a small NEW MEXICO town, Thor—a god living as man—walks slowly up a dusty street toward the Destroyer, which is breathing large gulfs of fire at everything in its way. Bystanders run for cover all around. **[Jesus—God living as a man—carries his cross slowly up a dusty street toward Golgotha, the place of his eventual crucifixion.]**

As Thor approaches his imminent death, he tells his brother listening from Asgard to leave the people around him alone. "Take mine and end this," he pleads. **[The night before, Jesus told the Roman soldiers who had come to arrest him, "I have already said that I am the One. If you are looking for Me, then let these men go free" (John 18:8).]**

The Destroyer steps back momentarily before taking a deadly swat at Thor, causing him to fly back about fifty feet. Jane runs to a dying Thor, who lies there struggling to breathe. "It's over," he tells her with his last bit of strength, before finally breathing out his last breath. **[Jesus, having hung on the cross for hours, can no longer hold himself up; therefore, breathing has become a near impossibility. "It is finished!" he finally says with his last bit of strength. "In that moment, His head fell; and He gave up the spirit" (John 19:30).]**

Far away in Asgard, Thor's father sheds a tear over the sacrifice of his son. Then Thor's hammer, which has been stuck in the ground fifty miles away, suddenly flies out of the ground at lightning speed straight for Thor, who miraculously sticks his hand up to catch the hammer just as it approaches him. Thor, suddenly alive and well, is immediately clothed in armor and royalty as he turns toward the Destroyer.

Jane stands there in awe, struggling for the right words to say. All she can manage is, "Oh . . . my . . . God." **[When Mary Magdalene and Mary first see Jesus after his resurrection, they take hold of his feet and worship the risen Messiah (Matt. 28:9).]**

The weather surrounding the immediate area grows dark. Wind, thunder, and lightning surround as Thor battles the Destroyer, leading quickly to its destruction. **[At the empty tomb, where death was finally defeated, there was an earthquake, and an angel of the Lord stood. His appearance we are told was like lightning (Matt. 28:2–3).]**

The death and resurrection of Thor, as depicted in the movie, bares some interesting commonalities with Jesus' death and resurrection. But perhaps any on-screen depiction of a resurrection would bare the same similarities. After all, in all of history we have only one sacrificial death and resurrection to look to for inspiration. (But I'm pretty sure he didn't ride in a chariot pulled by goats.)

Guess Who Said It First:
THE THINGS WE SAY THAT YOU NEVER KNEW WERE

▶ Spider-Man may have claimed to have "escaped by the skin of my teeth" from Doctor Octopus a few times, but did you know he was quoting the Old Testament figure Job?

"My bone cleaveth to my skin and to my flesh, and I am escaped with the skin of my teeth." (Job 19:20 KJV)

▶ Superman considers defeating armed robbers a "drop in the bucket," much like God considers Israel's enemies.

"Behold, the nations are as a drop of a bucket, and are counted as the small dust of the balance." (Isa. 40:15 KJV)

SUPERHERO VERSUS **SAVIOR**

I'm no fool. Please don't think I believe Hollywood's finest writers, directors, and producers sat in church pews drinking grape juice while listening to Amy Grant (after opening prayers led by Rick Warren, of course) and conspired together how they might be able to preach the gospel under the guise of superhero movies. Let's be honest—these superhero movies were made with one intention: making money. Christopher Nolan's Dark Knight trilogy made $1.2 billion (yes, billion with a *b*!) in ticket sales in the United States alone. Marvel's *The Avengers* made about half that all by itself. Superheroes on the big screen means hashtag trends on Twitter, Happy Meal toys that every kid must have, and more Jujyfruits sold at the concession stands.

So maybe these movies aren't being put out to represent Christ and to spread the gospel. But what if they represent something else of equal importance? What if, intentionally or not, consciously or subconsciously, these movies and their extreme popularity are telling us what the world truly needs?

The SUPERHERO Savior QUIZ

1. Jesus miraculously broke just a few loaves of bread and fishes and fed five thousand men, plus women and children. How many loaves and fishes did he start with?
   a. 3 loaves and 2 fishes
   b. 2 loaves and 3 fishes
   c. 3 cloves and 2 dishes
   d. 5 loaves and 2 fishes
   e. 2 loaves and 5 fishes

2. In John's account of the feeding of the five thousand, which two disciples were involved in Jesus' discussion of how to proceed?
   a. Peter and John
   b. Matthew and Thomas
   c. James and John
   d. Phillip and Andrew
   e. Simon and Garfunkel

The world certainly doesn't think we need a Messiah, but we do need Jor-El's only son, sent to earth to be the hope for all. The world may not believe it needs Jesus to be anything more than a good teacher, but we do need Spider-Man, choosing to be a hero at the sacrifice of living as a normal kid. Sure, this self-made world that chooses its own fate doesn't need a scapegoat Savior to take their punishment, but it does need an innocent Dark Knight to willingly take the blame for others' actions. And maybe the world thinks it doesn't need Jesus the sacrificial lamb, only Thor, who willingly gave up his life so others could live.

Maybe Hollywood isn't using superhero movies to tell us about Jesus but instead is telling those of us who know the true Superhero that *they* need him.

3. Who/what did the disciples think Jesus was when he walked across the water to their boat?
  a. An angel
  b. A ghost
  c. A sea creature
  d. Himself
  e. Someone who had inhaled way too
     much helium

4. After Jesus raised Jairus's daughter from the dead, what advice did he give those attending her? (two answers)
  a. "Tell no one what has happened."
  b. "Take the girl to the temple, and worship your heavenly Father."
  c. "Send the mourners away."
  d. "Give her something to eat."
  e. "Give her two aspirin, and call me in the morning."

5. Whose severed ear did Jesus heal when the chief priests came to appre-
hend him?

    a. One of the chief priests'

    b. Peter's

    c. The servant of the high priest

    d. A Roman soldier's

Answers: 1) d 2) d 3) b 4) a,d 5) c

CHAPTER 2

IMPERFECT *Movies,* PERFECT GOD

In early 2014, biblical epics *Son of God* and *Noah* stormed the big screen and found success, thanks in large part to the curiosity of churchgoers wondering how these biblical stories would be portrayed by Hollywood. Echoing how *The Passion of the Christ* found great success roughly a decade earlier, these movies were also previewed by multiple Christian audiences beforehand and marketed to churches who were given the opportunity to purchase tickets for their entire congregations.

Movies based on biblical stories tend to be one of two types of movies the conservative North American church supports in big ways, with the other type being the Christian-produced, Christian-directed, Christian-starred, Christian-catered, low-budget films that plaster the walls and shelves of Christian bookstores with posters and high-priced DVDs.

If a perfect God chose to use imperfect people to spread his gospel message, why can't he do the same with imperfect movies?

But are those the only two types of movies in which we can find biblical themes and redeeming qualities? Is the remaining 99 percent only filled with mindless entertainment at best and disgusting debauchery at worst?

Scratch that question. Answer this one instead: If a perfect God chose to use imperfect people to spread his gospel message (lest we forget adulterous David, doubting Thomas, prideful James and John, and countless others filling every page of the Bible), why can't he do the same with imperfect movies?

Biblical epics serve an awesome purpose of introducing the unchurched to amazing stories they may have never heard, which hopefully point many to reading the eternal Word for the first time in their lives. Even in a movie such as *Noah*, where there are significant differences from the Genesis story, at least it provides opportunity for dialogue and a reason for someone to open up Grandma's dusty King James Bible to find out more about Noah.

And the church support of recent Christian-produced movies such as *God's Not Dead* and *Courageous* have helped attribute to box office returns that can't be ignored, not even by Hollywood's standards (an estimated $61 million and $34 million in US ticket sales alone, respectively, not counting overseas box offices or DVD sales).

But there is so much more Hollywood is putting out that can be redeemed for God, if only viewers could see past the flaws and not demand biblical perfection from imperfect, perhaps unchurched filmmakers. And better yet, the unchurched world sees these movies in droves and is ripe for meaningful dialogue about what they just saw. But if the church does not see these movies, who will fill in the blanks and answer the questions many are asking as they walk out of the theaters?

Many such films come out every year, but the following is just a brief breakdown of three films from this century that have flaws as well as their fair share of bad language and other questionable content . . . just as all of us have too.

BRUCE **ALMIGHTY**

Synopsis: A man who complains too much about God is given the Almighty's powers to teach him a few lessons about what it takes to run the world.

Crude or profane language: One F-word, several S-words and other offensive words; multiple exclamatory uses of the Lord's name.

Sexual content: An unmarried man and woman live together and presumably have sex. There is one inappropriate scene where the woman is primping for their encounter, thrashing around and falling to the floor.

> **"The protagonist has a sexual relationship with a woman who isn't his wife. That's difficult to show support to."**

Yep. Welcome to Hollywood. Like it or not, keeping sex within the covenant of marriage is near impossible to find in movies and television these days, no matter how young the stars are. (One exception, strangely enough, is the *Twilight* saga. Apparently Edward's family still taught good old-fashioned values.) Indeed, Bruce and his girlfriend live together unrepentantly, and presumably have for a long time, despite the audience and Bruce finding out later that she has an active prayer life.

But are inappropriate sexual relationships among God's protagonists also found in the Bible, or are they contained only to the immoralities of Hollywood? Let's see: Abraham and Hagar, David and Bathsheba, Solomon and three hundred concubines, Rahab the prostitute (whom, incidentally, God used in the lineage of Jesus). . . . So yes. Not to mention many men with multiple wives. (The same Solomon also had seven hundred wives!)

That is not an argument to say that they were right, or that they never repented, or that those relationships were not in direct disobedience to God. Just that they are there in the Bible, found among good men and women whom God still used for his purposes.

> **"It's outrageous! Bruce used God's powers to do such things as finding Jimmy Hoffa's corpse and using a gust of wind to blow up a woman's skirt!"**

Yes, that is right. He also used his new abilities to enlarge his girlfriend's breasts, get his dog to use the toilet, bring the moon closer to the earth, and something involving a monkey and a gang member's rear end. Yes, Bruce took full, blasphemous advantage of having the power of God.

But look also at Moses, whom God had given the power to do such miracles as transforming Aaron's staff into a snake, turning water into blood, and using ashes from the furnace to bring boils upon the Egyptians. Later in the desert, God commanded him to strike a rock with his staff, and—voila!—enough water flowed from the rock to quench the thirst of all the Israelites. I suppose that one was Moses' favorite trick, because at a later time when God commanded him to simply speak to a rock in order for water to flow out, Moses became a little power hungry and decided he would strike the rock again. Unfortunately, unlike in the fictional world, this defiant act did not exactly sit well with God and had consequences: "Because you didn't trust Me and treat Me as holy before the Israelites, you will not lead this group into the land I have given them" (Num. 20:12).

> **"I lost forty-seven pounds on the Krispy Kreme diet!"**[1]
>
> —A woman whose prayer to God (Bruce) was answered just the way she asked

> **We have the opportunity every day to show Jesus to the world simply in how we live and how we love others, not only in the words we say.**

Then there are the men of the Bible whom God established as kings but who used their royal influence for their own pleasure and purposes, such as David having Uriah killed in battle in order to cover up his mistake with Bathsheba and Solomon building places of worship for the false gods of his foreign wives. And just keep on reading through the stories of the kings to find one after another misusing his power and influence for his own benefit.

There is a reason why God did not want to establish the kingship in Israel and why Jesus only gave his powers temporarily to a few select men: we can't handle having that power, nor can we be trusted to only do good with it. Not Bruce. And not you or me.

"There's no mention of Jesus in the movie."

True. Outside of profanities, the words "Jesus," "Messiah," "Son of God," or any other reference to the Savior cannot be found in the movie. To further the point, when Morgan Freeman's God character talks about real miracles (as opposed to when Bruce parted his tomato soup á la Moses and the Red Sea), he mentions only single moms raising a family and teenagers choosing education over drugs, while ignoring the ultimate miracle of Jesus' resurrection. However, one also cannot find the name "Jesus" in the New Testament book of 3 John, or even a single reference to God in the Old Testament book of Esther. Certainly no one is calling for those books to be thrown out of the Bible or thinks they cannot be used for God's purposes.

But perhaps there is a vivid picture of Jesus shown throughout the movie, not to be realized until the very end. Multiple

Bruce: "How do you make someone love you without affecting free will?"
God: "Welcome to my world, son. You come up with an answer to that one, you let me know."[2]

"I'm done. Please. I don't want to do this anymore. I don't want to be God. I want you to decide what's right for me. I surrender to your will!"[3]

—Bruce, speaking for anyone who has thought they could do a better job with their life than God

times in the film, Bruce sees a homeless man on the street holding signs that say things like "R EWE BLIND," "LIFE IS JUST," and "GOD BEE GOOD HONEY." In one scene during the movie's final act, Bruce is stuck in traffic and notices two people: one is the homeless man holding a new sign that says "ALL FOR WON" and the second is a man stranded on the road next to his broken-down car. Bruce takes it upon himself to pull over and help the driver push his car to the side of the road, away from traffic. In the movie's final seconds, the homeless man is shown one more time. As the camera zooms in on his face, the homeless man transforms into Morgan Freeman, the actor who portrayed God in the film. An instant reminder of Jesus' words to his disciples: "Whenever you saw a brother *or sister hungry or cold*, whatever you did to the least of these, so you did to Me" (Matt. 25:40).

Jesus does not have to be mentioned by name in order to be referenced or modeled. Like Bruce helping the stranded driver, we have the opportunity every day to show Jesus to the world simply in how we live and how we love others, not only in the words we say. Why should a separate standard be applied to a two-hour Hollywood movie?

"What can we learn from this movie then?"

As is the case with many movies, most of the payoff in *Bruce Almighty* is in the end. Despite driving his dream car, getting the anchor job he always wanted, and basically being able to fulfill any desire he had, Bruce loses his girlfriend and realizes that without her he has nothing. He even tells her, "None of this seems right without you."[4] And when God confronts him and asks him to pray from his heart, to really ask for what he wants more than anything, Bruce admits all he wants is his girlfriend . . . Grace.

Names are not chosen randomly in movies and books, and the name chosen for Bruce's girlfriend is certainly no exception. Grace. As in, "Grace, none of this seems right without you." As in, Grace—the only thing Bruce wants in the end.

The apostle Paul would agree: "For it is by grace you have been saved, through faith—and this is not from yourselves, it is the gift of God" (Eph. 2:8 NIV). Indeed, grace is the greatest gift. Like Bruce, we are sinful, selfish people who have no way of saving ourselves or finding true happiness on our own. But as Paul said in 1 Corinthians 15:10: "By the grace of God I am what I am, and his grace to me was not without effect" (NIV). We are what we are, because of God's grace. Sinners made children of God, set to inherit his royal kingdom in heaven. Nothing else we may obtain or become matters if we don't have God's grace.

 SIGNS

Synopsis: A family finds mysterious crop circles in their fields, which bring fear of an impending alien invasion.

Crude or profane language: Several profanities and crude expressions. A teenager confesses to her former priest all the swear words she has said recently. A young child curses at his father in a moment of anger.

"The pastor who lost his faith does not show a Job-like strength in his relationship with God. Who's to say he won't lose it again when the next crisis comes?"

> "What you have to ask yourself is, what kind of person are you? Are you the kind who sees signs, sees miracles? Or do you believe that people just get lucky?"[6]
>
> —Graham, who no longer sees miracles

The man's wife was basically severed in half when she was hit by a car and pinned against a tree. Let's give him a break. Show me a man who lost the love of his life in such a fashion but doesn't struggle in his faith, and I'll show you a fictional character in a straight-to-DVD Christian film.

God does not look at snapshots of our lives and declare us as guilty or righteous based on what we show to him at that time. (Thank goodness!) Presumably, Graham, the protagonist of *Signs*, was a faithful minister many months before the movie takes place. When we meet him, however, he refuses to let anyone call him "Father," and says things to his family such as, "There is no one watching out for us. . . . We are all on our own."[5]

But a final glimpse of him wearing his clergy outfit has the implication that he has seen God working through the crises of his life.

Does one particular season in Graham's life declare him righteous before God and another season declare him unrighteous? No. "No one is righteous—not even one. There is no one who understands *the truth*; no one is seeking after the *one True* God. All have turned away; together they've become worthless. No one does good, not even one" (Rom. 3:10–12). What if we looked at this snapshot of the prophet Habakkuk's life: "How long must I cry, O Eternal One, and get no answer from You? Even when I yell to You, 'Violence *is all around*!' You do nothing to save *those in distress*" (Hab. 1:2)? Or how about this one, also from Habakkuk: "Why do You *stand by and* watch those who act treacherously? Why do You say *and do* nothing when the wicked swallows up one who is more in the right than he is?" (v. 13).

If we stopped at either of those places, we would've missed the last verses of Habakkuk's conversation with the Almighty: "Even if the fig tree does not blossom and there are no grapes on the vines, if the olive trees fail to give fruit and the fields produce no food, if the flocks die *far* from the fold and there are no cattle in the stalls; then I will *still* rejoice in the Eternal! I will rejoice in the God who saves me!" (3:17–18).

Perhaps Graham will once again falter when life brings another crisis. And maybe Habakkuk had more unpleasant words for God when the Babylonians eventually conquered the land in which he lived. It is human for the faith of the unrighteous to fluctuate, but thankfully we are "made righteous" (Rom. 5:19 NLT) by the one we place our faith in.

> **"Without any solid conclusion to the luck-versus-providence debate brought up in the film, the unchurched audience is left to make up their own decisions. They are never led to the Bible for answers."**

You're exactly right. If that had been the movie's mission statement, then one could say the movie failed. Except that it didn't, because that wasn't its mission. The director, producers, stars, and production company had one goal in mind with this movie: make money. And with an estimated budget of $72 million and a box office intake of $228 million, I would say it succeeded quite well.[7]

So if the movie doesn't bring the audience to the rightful conclusion that God, indeed, has a plan for each of our lives and is constantly weaving his intricate tapestry, how will they know?

Here's a thought. . . . Why don't *we* tell them?

Why would anyone ever insist that a movie should have all the answers laid out for its audience, when the only thing in the entire universe that has all the answers is God's message to us, given in the form of the Bible, and the way he

"I knew the second it happened it was a miracle. I could have been kissing her when she threw up. That would have scarred me for life. I may never have recovered. . . . I'm a miracle man."[8]

—Merrill, who may see too many things as miracles

chose to spread that message is through his people? If all a movie such as *Signs* does is ask the right questions, then we should all celebrate. Because in the Bible we have all the right answers.

"What can we learn from this movie then?"

Graham's son: "Did someone save me?"

Graham: "Yeah, I think Someone did."[9]

—When Graham finally acknowledged God's work in their lives

Graham Hess is a Christian to whom many can relate. Along with the already-mentioned tragedy in his life that is unfortunately all-too-common in this broken world we live in, we can also relate to his many imperfections. Graham struggles to be the leader and father his children need in their life. Perhaps this is evident also to his brother, Merrill, and why he moved in with the family. But Graham's love for them is unwavering, as is his dedication to protecting them during the impending alien invasion. So until he is able to regain the spiritual leadership he once had in the family, he will lead with his love and presence. And despite Graham's obvious struggles, his family does not give up on him either. The family unit is strong, despite the turmoil surrounding it.

The heartbreaking scene near the end when Graham refuses to pray before what he believes will be their last meal on earth reaches deep inside our sinful selves. Not many can compare to King David, who when fleeing possible death wrote, "My adversaries are many, too many to count. Now they have taken a stand against me! . . . I lift my voice to You, Eternal One" (Ps. 3:1, 4). Like Graham, we oftentimes struggle to speak to our Father while the hurricane is pounding down on our life, for doing so may force us to admit that we're not in control, and that we are helplessly at his mercy. But "God is good" (Ps. 73:1), for though "we are unfaithful, He remains faithful" (2 Tim. 2:13). Just as God never left Graham's side in that basement when Graham made it quite clear he was not welcome, he also will not give up on us when we are too weak or stubborn to call on him.

As is shown here at the end, as well as throughout the movie, there is clearly no joy in Graham's life, which one might immediately attribute to the loss of his wife. But since we're to assume it's shortly after his wife's death that Graham also left his position at the local church, could not the true reason for his loss of joy be in his refusal to walk with God? The psalmist wrote, "I keep my eyes always on the Lord. . . . You will fill me with joy in your presence, with eternal pleasures at your right hand" (Ps. 16:8, 11 NIV). God fills us with joy. Not a spouse. Not children. Not having a trial-free life. Only God is the source of true joy. And even when a family member dies, even when a world-ending catastrophe appears to be pending, Paul's instructions to the Philippians apply to Graham and the rest of us as well: "*Always* be full of joy in the Lord. . . . Don't worry about *anything*; instead, pray about everything. Tell God what you need, and thank him *for all* he has done. Then you will experience God's peace, which exceeds anything we can understand" (Phil. 4:4–7 NLT 1996, emphasis added). Graham had forgotten that despite all he had lost, he still had reason to find joy and the ability to experience peace. Perhaps the Graham we see just before the closing credits had finally come to terms with this truth.

Despite Graham's trouble leading his family, despite his wavering faith that led to a loss of joy, despite his stubbornness to acknowledge God and admit he was not in control of his life, God remained faithful until his prodigal son Graham returned to him. And he will do so again if needed.

THE BOOK OF **ELI**

Synopsis: A post-apocalyptic tale in which one man journeys across America in order to protect a sacred book from falling into the wrong hands.

Crude or profane language: Multiple F-words and S-words. A variety of other vulgarities, including taking God's name in vain.

Violence: Countless slashes and stabbings with a large knife, with a ridiculous amount of blood splatter. A woman is nearly raped before an arrow pierces her attacker in the worst of places. A cat is skewered in the opening scene.

"It is just too violent. How can this be a man of God?"

Indeed, the violence in this movie can be hard to watch at times. When Eli warns a man that if he lays his hand on Eli again he won't get it back, you just know that the following scene is going to make you cringe. For Eli was nothing if not a man of his word. However, all the violence and death Eli brings upon the people in his path is in self-defense. Each time he is approached, he attempts to walk on through without having to resort to violence.

This is Hollywood, however, and the audience paid to see Denzel Washington kick some post-apocalyptic butt, so that is what we get to see. But is it too much? Can Eli truly be a messenger of God while also being an angel of death?

If a movie were made out of the Old Testament Samson's life, would we not also be covering our eyes and telling young kids they need to be older before they can see it, if at all? Judges 15:15 may be the bloodiest verse in the Bible: "Grabbing up a fresh jawbone of a donkey, *he began fighting them* [the Philistines]. *That day* he killed 1,000 Philistines." One man, one donkey jawbone ("fresh" . . . eww), one thousand dead. Suddenly Eli's not quite so bad, is he?

And Samson wasn't just some crazy, fuel-enraged, steroids-pumping whacko who went on a killing spree. Verse 14 tells us that God gave Samson the strength to break free of his ropes so that he could fight the Philistines. And verses 16–17 say that immediately after the massacre, Samson sings—sings!—a "triumphant song."

Or in Judges 7 (Judges is a pretty violent book, it turns out), how PG do you think it was when Gideon and his army of three hundred rushed the Midianites, causing tens of thousands to "turn on each other with their swords"

> "Cursed be the ground for our sake. Both thorns and thistles it shall bring forth for us. For out of the ground we were taken, for the dust we are, and to the dust we shall return."[10]
>
> —Eli, paraphrasing Genesis 3:17–19 just before he introduces an entire roomful to his special blade.

Having seen *The Book of Eli* multiple times now, I am still convicted that I don't treat the Bible nearly as sacred as this movie upholds it.

(v. 22 NIV)? The enemy didn't hold their breaths until they quietly fell down out of suffocation; tens of thousands purposely fell on each other's swords because that seemed to be the better way to die.

The mighty David, long before he became king, took down a giant Philistine with one rock and a slingshot. "That's not so bad," you might say. "Children are told that story all the time." Of course they are. Everyone who grew up going to Sunday school knows the story of David and Goliath. But conveniently most teachers and parents stop the 1 Samuel 17 story at verse 50: "That was how David defeated the Philistine with only a sling and a *single* stone, striking him down, ending his life without a sword in his hand." Hooray for David! One stone. No sword. Minimal bloodshed.

But read on: "Then David ran to the Philistine and stood over his *lifeless* body. He pulled the man's sword from its scabbard and finished him by cutting off his head" (v. 51).

He ran.

To the dead body.

And cut off his head.

With a giant's sword that was probably so heavy it acted as more of a saw than a sword for David's endeavor.

Yes, Eli is a violent man of God. But in a world with no law or government, he must decide between allowing street gangs to rob and murder him or fighting back, believing that he is doing so with the authority of God because of the mission he has been sent on. Perhaps he should've had the faith that Jacob's mother, Rebekah, was also lacking when she did not trust that Jacob would receive his father's blessing unless she deceptively intervened (Gen. 27). But just as God still used Rebekah, he remained faithful to Eli as well during his journey despite the blood he left behind him in his path.

"In the end, the Bible is simply placed on a shelf between the Jewish Torah and the Islamic Quran. Apparently, after all this time, it was no more important than those books."

Not so fast. In Exodus 7, when Pharaoh's magicians turned their staffs into snakes, that certainly did not nullify the miracle of Moses and Aaron doing the same thing. And just because the witch of Endor was able to bring forth the spirit of Samuel to consult with King Saul (1 Sam. 28), that does not minimize the moment when long-deceased Moses and Elijah appeared on the mountain to witness Jesus' transfiguration.

Don't forget. This amazing journey portrayed in *The Book of Eli* was about the Bible. Not the Torah or the Quran. Not the works of Shakespeare, Nietzsche, or J. K. Rowling, but the Bible, the eternal Word of God. We are not told how any of the other books in this Alcatraz library were found and preserved for the new world, but it's a safe assumption that God did not lead a man to the only remaining copy in all the world and guide him on a thirty-year journey west while keeping him safe from street gangs whose bullets seemed to miss him a bit too often. (And yes, I'm keeping the final secret an actual secret, unlike some spoiler-filled reviews I read. Shame on you! Did you also tell your readers that Bruce Willis was dead the whole time in *The Sixth Sense*? Oops . . .)

> **"Walk by faith, not by sight."**[11]
>
> —Eli, quoting the apostle Paul, when Solara asks him how he knows he's on the right mission

The antagonist Carnegie is not looking for any other book to use for his personal glorification. Since he is older like Eli, he knows of the Bible from when he was a kid and the power that it has. "It's a weapon!" he says. "People will come from all over. They'll do exactly what I tell them if the words are from the book."[12] He isn't interested in using the Torah or Quran as a weapon. Only the Bible. Though his motivation in finding and sharing the Bible is clearly evil, even he knows the Bible stands above all other books.

What happens with the spread of the Bible after the events of the movie, we do not know. It's fiction. But the message still is that God didn't send Eli on a thirty-year journey to improve his cardio, nor did he allow countless lives to be slaughtered by his messenger because they were no more valuable than swine being brought down by Angry Birds. In *The Book of Eli*, God took great lengths to ensure the survival of his Book, and he will be just as purposeful about the spreading of its message.

"What can we learn from this movie then?"

Having seen the movie multiple times now, I am still convicted that I don't treat the Bible nearly as sacred as this movie upholds it. Whether it's paperback or leather-bound, NIV or KJV, with commentary or without, the pages that hold the eternal, "God-breathed" Word (2 Tim. 3:16) contain the only earthly possession man cannot live without. Yet if I were a contestant on *Survivor*, the one personal possession I would take with me would be ChapStick.

But Eli reads from the Bible every day. He quotes it often, even before a fight. "It's not just a book," he tells young Solara. And to Eli, that's undoubtedly true. The Bible is his daily strength. It's his mission. And he will protect it no matter the cost. The takeaway is that all God's children should value the Bible as Eli does.

Just as Jesus' message of salvation would have died with him if his disciples had not followed his command to "go out and make disciples in all the nations. . . . *Form them in the practices and postures that* I have taught you, and show them how to follow the commands I have laid down for you" (Matt. 28:19–20), so perhaps would the Bible in *The Book of Eli* if not for Eli's disciple, Solara.

Eli meets Solara in the town that the evil Carnegie presides over with a Hitler-like dictatorship, and though he does not tell her, "Follow me," as Jesus did with his disciples,

"Pay close attention, and write down everything I say, exactly as I say it."[13]

—Eli to his transcriber, perhaps reminiscent of what God told Moses just before he began dictating to him on Mount Sinai she joins Eli on his mission nonetheless. He teaches her to pray before a meal (which she immediately teaches to her mother) and reads aloud Scripture at night. Her first introduction to the Word is Psalm 23, which she surely dwells on the next day as she "walks though the valley of the shadow of death" and chooses to "fear no evil" as she rolls a live grenade under Carnegie's truck.

When Solara tells Eli that she hates the town she lives in, he tells her, "Then change it." In the final scene, Solara packs up her things, presumably armed with a newly printed Bible, and heads back home. To change it, as the original disciples did.

Guess Who Said It First:
THE THINGS WE SAY THAT YOU NEVER KNEW WERE
from the Bible

▶ Bruce may have been thinking it when all his selfish deeds came back to haunt him, but the apostle Paul said it first:

"For whatsoever a man soweth, that shall he also reap." (Gal. 6:7 KJV)

▶ If only Eli's foes had ever found and read the Bible. They would have known Jesus' warning that "whoever lives by the sword, dies by the sword."

"Then said Jesus unto him, Put up again thy sword into his place: for all they that take the sword shall perish with the sword." (Matt. 26:52 KJV)

I have a friend who used to say, "Why are we surprised when a non-Christian acts like a non-Christian?" By the same token, why do we act surprised when imperfect people make imperfect movies? Even worse, why don't we support their heroic (yes, heroic) efforts to try and put meaningful content on the big screen that could result in planting the seeds necessary to changing lives? Because without our support of these films, the Christians attributing to the production of them could end up being replaced by those only concerned with making the next popcorn flick or sex romp.

There are also many other movies released each year that may not have some of the more obvious and intentional biblical themes as the ones detailed in this chapter, yet the allegories in them are begging for dialogue. Movies such as *Frozen*, *The Hunger Games*, and the Harry Potter series are centered on stories of sacrifice. Anytime one person, fictional or not, is willing to give up his life for another, we are left with the message of the gospel.

Though the depiction of the afterlife in *The Sixth Sense* does not correspond with what the Bible shares with us, the climactic moment when we learn that the protagonist was dead but did not know it is a reminder of Ephesians 2, when the apostle Paul shares, "As for you, *don't you remember how you used to just exist? Corpses,* dead *in life,* buried by transgressions, wandering the course of this *perverse* world. *You were the offspring* of the prince of the power of air—*oh, how he owned you,* just as he still controls those living in disobedience" (vv. 1–2). In short, those still living without Jesus and chained to their sins are dead and don't even know it.

And movies such as *The Matrix* and *Minority Report* are filled with thought-provoking themes like captivity disguised as freedom and free will versus predestination. The famous Hollywood names behind these movies may not always be the preferred entertainers of the church crowd, but that doesn't mean the content in their movies cannot be redeemed for eternity.

Do not interpret anything I've said in this chapter to mean everyone's next family movie night needs to be in front of *The Book of Eli*. That would be way, way inappropriate. I even remember seeing kids in the theater for *The Passion of the Christ* and questioning their parents' reasons for bringing them to see the movie. But my support of movies such as the ones I've spoken of here is not about ministering to and sharing the good news of Christ with my children. Hopefully all parents can do that effectively without having to show their children a movie first—"Okay, Junior, how do you think you would respond if your wife's body were severed by a car?" Instead it's about relating with the people who are spending fifty to one hundred million dollars in the movie's first week to go see it. Your coworkers. Your neighbors.

Your mission field.

The R-RATED OLD TESTAMENT QUIZ

1. When were twenty-four young men slain in combat just before a battle?
    a. When a tournament of champions was held before the battle between the forces of Ishbosheth and the forces of David.
    b. When David and his brothers killed Goliath and his men.
    c. When Goliath killed the champions of Israel.
    d. When Samson smote the Philistines.

2. Who actually killed the Midianite army?
    a. God, with fire and hailstones from heaven.
    b. Gideon's men, with the element of surprise.
    c. An army of Ammonites, who, unbeknownst to Gideon, were waiting in the hills where the Midianites fled.
    d. Themselves.
    e. Troops whom Gideon had sent back to camp.

3. What was the first evidence of God's enhancement of Samson's strength?
    a. He killed thirty Philistines.
    b. He bench-pressed Goliath fifteen times.
    c. He killed a young lion without any kind of weapon.
    d. He knocked over part of a city wall at the outskirts of Philistia.
    e. He uprooted a large tree with his bare hands.

4. How did Samson destroy the fields of the Philistines, along with their vineyards and olive groves?

    a. He dragged two large trees through the fields, for two entire days without ceasing.

    b. He stampeded five thousand cattle throughout the fields and vineyards until everything was destroyed.

    c. He filled fifteen hollow tree logs with locusts, and plugged each end of the logs with the carcasses of thirty lions he had killed. Then he dragged the trees to the Philistine fields and released the locusts.

    d. He collected three hundred foxes and tied their tails together in pairs. Then he set their tails on fire and released them in the fields.

    e. He attacked them with "Greek fire."

5. What weapon did Samson use to slay one thousand Philistines, according to Judges 15?

    a. A donkey's jawbone

    b. The femur (leg bone) of a lion

    c. A large tree branch

    d. A scourge (a whip with metal fragments attached to it)

Answers: 1) a 2) d 3) c 4) d 5) a

The apostle Paul wrote:

I've made a life outside the law to gather those who live outside the law (although I personally abide by and live under the Anointed One's law). I've been *broken, lost, depressed, oppressed, and* weak that I might *find favor and* gain the weak. I'm *flexible, adaptable, and* able to do and be whatever is needed for all kinds of people so that *in the end* I can use every means at my disposal to offer them salvation. I do it all for the gospel *and for the hope* that I may participate with everyone who is blessed by the proclamation of the good news. (1 Cor. 9:21–23)

What if being "flexible, adaptable, and able to . . . use every means at my disposal to offer them salvation" included using flawed movies made by flawed people?

CHAPTER 3

EVERYTHING *Awesome!* IS (WHEN YOU KNOW YOU'RE **A CHILD OF A KING)**

At perhaps no other time in the history of animation has it been as cool to be a movie-going kid as it is today. Or the kid's parents. Or the big brother and sister. Or simply anyone who loves the movies.

Not too long ago the options for family-friendly animated movies consisted of orphan dinosaurs traveling the world in *The Land Before Time*, a tiny girl with a fairy prince in *Thumbelina*, and emigrating mice in *An American Tail*. Basically, "family friendly" really meant "young child friendly," and big brother was wondering how long he could sneak into the latest *Friday the 13th* movie while pretending to go buy some Sno-Caps.

But in November 1995, Pixar Animation Studios gave the whole family the gift that keeps on giving when they introduced to the world Woody, Buzz Lightyear, and the rest of the gang in *Toy Story*. Suddenly the bar had been raised, not just with the incredible computer animation but also with the stories, characters, and humor that appealed to all generations. Pixar would later

*Everyone is uniquely created by a God who cares recklessly
and without abandon for them.*

give us additional box-office blockbusters such as *Monsters, Inc.*, *The Incredibles*, and *Up*, which led to other studios getting in on the newfound popularity with their own intergenerational animated movies—*Shrek*, *Despicable Me*, *Bee Movie*, and *Monsters vs. Aliens*, to name just a few.

Along with a who's who in Hollywood list of voice actors that includes Steve Carrell, Nicholas Cage, Queen Latifah, Brad Pitt, Jack Black, and countless more, this new generation of animated films also bring with them relatable stories and themes that inspire young kids, produce meaningful dialogue on Twitter and blogs, and might even cause a few adults to fight back a tear or two. Characters with names like Gru, Wyldstyle, Eep, and Flynn Rider have stories to tell that parallel truths told long ago by the Bible's Isaiah, David, John, Paul, and Jesus himself about who each of us truly is: children of God meant to live in the freedom of Jesus, the Light of the World.

 DESPICABLE ME **NO MORE**

In the 2010 film *Despicable Me*, Agnes, Edith, and Margo are three sisters who have spent far too long in Miss Hattie's Home for Girls. After spending all day trying to sell enough cookies for Miss Hattie so as to not be forced to spend the weekend in the box of shame, young Agnes asks Miss Hattie what we can only assume she asks her at the end of most days: "Anybody come to adopt us while we were out?"[1]

Every day, at the forefront of Agnes and her sisters' minds was, "Did anyone come to rescue us and give us a home, a family, a purpose?" Not dinner. Not school. Not the newest iTunes app. Their only concern was, "Does someone love me enough to call me his own?"

According to a recent US Department of Health and Human Services report, there are roughly one hundred thousand children in the United States foster care system on any given day waiting to be adopted. And an estimated four hundred thousand children total go through the system each year,[2] all scared yet anxious to ask at the end of each day the same question as Agnes: "Anybody come to adopt us while we were out?"

But orphans are by no means the only people in the world today not feeling as though they are cherished members of a family. Sons and daughters of all ages still seek a further sense of family, of being needed in society, of being noticed as the special creations they are. *Despicable Me*'s antihero, Gru, who would initially adopt the girls only to use them as a part of his diabolical plan to shrink and steal the moon, grew up with a mom at home who failed to nurture and encourage him. She never believed in any of his invention ideas, and when he told her upon watching the Apollo moon landing on television that he wanted to go to the moon one day as well, she told him it was too late—NASA was no longer sending monkeys to space.

Whether one is an actual orphan like Agnes and her sisters, or an emotional one like Gru, everyone is uniquely created by a God who cares recklessly and without abandon for them. He would be the first to follow them on Twitter, as well as their first friend on Facebook, and he would even keep checking back on their long-abandoned MySpace pages to see if they had finally been updated. God cares about every intricate detail of our lives, and he has gone out of his way to let us know that.

When Moses came down from the mountain to share with the Israelites the law that God had given him, he said of the Lord, "He enforces His justice for *the powerless, such as* orphans and widows" (Deut. 10:18), and then an additional ten times in the law given in Deuteronomy God specifically calls out the orphans and the widows as those to be especially loved and protected. And in Psalm 68, David sings praises to God because he is "a father to the fatherless" (v. 5).

And for the Grus of the world, who already have a home and a family, their Creator still wants them to know that he "decided in advance to adopt us into his own family by bringing us to himself through Jesus Christ. This is what he wanted to do, and it gave him great pleasure" (Eph. 1:5 NLT). And Galatians 4:5 says that God sent his only Son, Jesus, to purchase our freedom for us, "so that he could adopt us as his very own children" (NLT).

If only all God's children knew they had a Father in him who sacrificed so much for their sake. For everyone like Agnes who prays at night that "someone will adopt us soon, and that the mommy and daddy will be nice," or for those like Gru who want to finally know what it is like to be truly loved, God says, "Come to Me" (Matt. 11:28). Come to your Father.

ONE DISNEY PRINCESS MOVIE WE'LL NEVER SEE— JEZEBEL: DOG LOVER

- ▶ Daughter of King Ethbaal of the Sidonians

- ▶ Married King Ahab, who was "more wicked than all the wicked kings who lived before him" (1 Kings 16:30)

- ▶ Tried to kill all of God's prophets

- ▶ Supported prophets of false gods

- ▶ Threatened God's prophet Elijah: "May the gods kill me and worse, if I haven't killed you the way you killed their priests by this time tomorrow. *Your end is near, Elijah*." (1 Kings 19:2)

- ▶ Framed an innocent man and had him stoned to death so that her husband could have the man's vineyard

- ▶ Trampled to death by horses and eaten by dogs (Look it up! The gruesome tale is found in 2 Kings 9.)

IN THE **DARK** WITH THE **CROODS**

"Most days we spent in our cave, in the dark. Night after night. Day after day. . . . Anything new was bad. Curiosity is bad. Going out at night is bad. Basically, anything fun is bad."[3]

The opening monologue from cave girl Eep in the 2013 film *The Croods* sets up the background for this prehistoric family led by father Grug, who in order to keep them all safe has raised his children with the belief that "new is always bad" and wonders things like, "How could she not like the cave? It's so cozy."[4]

Eep's younger brother, Thunk, has bought into his dad's philosophy. "I get it, Dad. I get it. I will never do anything new or different,"[5] he tells his father, incredibly without an ounce of sarcasm in his voice. But teenage Eep has become no longer content with her family's rules. She's itching to get out of the cave and spend some time in the light of day discovering the world around them. One night, she sees a light flickering through a crack in the cave and wonders how there could be light in the darkness. And an adventure of discovery begins. Out of the darkness and into the light.

Even those who were once orphans but have been adopted into God's family can feel a false sense of security by remaining in the darkness at times. Like Grug, who still screamed out, "We need a cave!"[6] even when he found himself in an exciting new jungle filled with wildlife and beauty he had never seen before, we can forget that we "are all children of the light and of the day; we don't belong to darkness and night" (1 Thess. 5:5 NLT). Paul's warning to the church in Ephesus is a reminder for us as well: "If you have heard Jesus and have been taught by Him according to the truth that is in Him, then you know to take off your former way of life, your *crumpled* old self" (Eph. 4:21–22). But Grug found great comfort in the cave, just as we can feel safe in the familiarity of the darkness, not able to see the chains still on our hands and feet. However, we are told, "If you are walking in darkness, without a ray of light, trust in the LORD and rely on your God" (Isa. 50:10 NLT). But he is not in the darkness; rather, "God is in the light" (1 John 1:7 NLT).

And in the light is exactly where Eep wanted to be. For her, that night in the cave when she saw a strange light, Isaiah's prophecy rang true: "For those who live in a land of deep darkness, a light will shine" (Isa. 9:2 NLT). And so she followed the light in the darkness, which led her to a boy named Guy, who in turn led her family in an adventure that saved them from the imperilment disguised as contentment.

Eep was right to follow her notions. God intended his children to "act like children of the light" (Eph. 5:8). And rule number one for living in the light is an obvious yet necessary statement: stay away from the caves. We must give up our former ways of life, from before we knew who we were as children of God. We must not live behind the seemingly impenetrable boulder of Satan's lie that tells us we belong in the darkness, that someone as beautiful and righteous and perfect as God would not want us in the light with him. And finally, we must not give in to the temptation to remain chained to the laws of the cave. When Grug tries convincing Eep that the rules kept them alive, she tells him, "That wasn't living! That was just not dying. There's a difference."[7]

The apostle Paul would agree: "Christ has truly set us free. Now make sure that you stay free, and don't get tied up again in slavery to the law" (Gal. 5:1 NLT). We have been made free from the dark; how can we live in it any longer (Rom. 6:2)? Grug finally comes to terms with this: "No more dark. No more hiding. No more caves."[8] As should all of us.

Eep began their story by explaining that her family spent most of their days in the darkness of a cave, which unfortunately describes many people walking on earth today. But her final words in sharing their story point to a new direction, one God desires for all of his children: "From now on, we'll stay out here, where we can follow the light."[9]

Jesus spoke to the people once more and said, "I am the light of the world. If you follow me, you won't have to walk in darkness, because you will have the light that leads to life" (John 8:12 NLT).

We must give up our former ways of life, from before we knew who we were as children of God.

THE PARABLE OF the Lost Queen

If Luke 15 had a fourth "lost" parable, it might have gone something like the plot of Disney's *Frozen*:

There once was a princess who would one day become queen. Born with the power to create ice and snow, she was told she was a danger to others. "Conceal it. Don't feel it. Don't let it show,"[10] her father told her as a young girl. So she spent her childhood isolated from the world, even her family, until the day of her coronation when she accidentally reveals her curse to the entire kingdom.

Ashamed and embarrassed, the new queen leaves her kingdom to isolate herself at the top of a mountain. "I belong here. Alone. Where I can be who I am without hurting anybody," she says.[11]

But her sister, Anna, goes after the queen, wanting to bring her home. Daring the danger of the snow and mountains, Anna refuses to return home without her sister. Despite being told that most people who disappear into the mountains want to be alone, she says, "Nobody wants to be alone," and continues on.[12]

When Anna finds the queen, she begs her to come home again. "You don't have to live in fear," she tells her.[13] But the queen refuses, knowing the danger she is to her sister as well as to others. "There's no escape from the storm inside of me," she tries to tell Anna. "I can't control the curse."[14]

Though the queen resists her sister and tries to keep herself isolated, Anna does not give up, leading to the ultimate act of true love—sacrificing her life for her sister's. With Anna's sacrifice and resurrection, the queen's curse is broken, and the endless winter comes to an end.

(For more on curses and sacrificial love, watch *Frozen* . . . or read the Bible.)

NOT YOUR **AVERAGE LEGO**

Emmet is no one special. He wakes up at the same time each day and follows all the same instructions ("Step one . . . Breathe"[15]). He goes to his construction job where he continuously destroys and builds, destroys and builds, destroys and builds. He drinks overpriced coffee and watches his favorite TV show, *Where Are My Pants?*, alone with his plants. His neighbors and coworkers say about him, "He's kind of an average, normal kinda guy" and, "We all have something that makes us something, and Emmet is . . . nothing."[16] Even Batman tells him, "You are so disappointing on so many levels."[17] Yes, Emmet is no one special.

Except he is. He just hasn't been told it yet.

So when he meets the beautiful Wyldstyle, who looks into his eyes and says, "You're the special. . . . You are the most important, most talented, most interesting, and most extraordinary person in the universe,"[18] Emmet takes off on a mission to save the world on Taco Tuesday from the evil Lord Business and his kra-gl-e. With the confidence that comes with his newfound identity, Emmet leads Batman, Princess Unikitty, Wyldstyle, and others into battle in order to save all of Bricksburg.

All because he was finally told who he was.

If Emmet, whose greatest idea at this point in his life had been the double-decker couch, could save all of Bricksburg, what if all of us were finally told how special, important, interesting, and extraordinary we are . . . and we believed it?

Because the Word of God tells us that, in Jesus Christ, we are all:

- children of God (John 1:12)
- friends of Jesus (John 15:15)
- belonging to God (1 Cor. 6:20)
- established, anointed, and sealed by God (2 Cor. 1:21–22)
- citizens of heaven (Phil. 3:20)

- forgiven (Col. 1:14)

- God's coworkers (2 Cor. 6:1)

- God's handiwork (Eph. 2:10)

- completed by God (Phil 1:6)

- strong in the Lord (Eph. 6:10)

- not alone (Heb. 13:5)

- victorious (1 John 5:4)

- no longer condemned (Rom. 8:1–2)

- new creations (2 Cor. 5:17)

And so much more.

It may look as though we are all alone, yet we are not. We may feel condemned, yet that is not true either. Satan tells us we are not forgiven, but he is lying. We may not feel as though we belong anywhere, with anyone; however, we belong to God and have an eternal home in heaven waiting for us. Though we feel weak at times, know that God makes us strong. And the world might be showing us a big, fat *L* with their hand, but we can be assured that we are victorious, because our Father has overcome the world.

How would it look to live your life with the confidence of these truths concerning your identity? How would your seemingly average, normal, everyday life be different? Because God is saying to you, "You're the special."

But of course, Emmet finds out that the prophecy Vitruvius said about him was made up. When he learns this, he tells Wyldstyle that when she had told him he was special, talented, and important, "That was the first time anyone had ever really told me that. And it made me want to do everything I could to be the guy you were talking about."[19]

However, it didn't matter to Emmet that the prophecy had been made up. He knew now that it was still true about him, just as it was also true about Lord Business. Emmet would later share with Business almost word for word what Wyldstyle once told him: "You are the most talented, most interesting, and most extraordinary person in the universe. And you are capable of amazing things, because you are the special. And so am I. And so is everyone."[20]

Five times the gospel writer John referred to himself as "the disciple whom Jesus loved" (John 13:23; 19:26; 20:2; 21:7, 20 NIV). In no way was John insinuating that Jesus did not love the other disciples; he knew they were all loved equally. But John was sure of his identity in Jesus and lived his life with the comfort and confidence that came with it. He knew that he was "the disciple whom Jesus loved." As were Peter, Matthew, James, and all of us to this day.

Emmet wasn't blowing smoke in Lord Business's ears when he told him he was the most extraordinary person in the universe. It was the complete truth. As it was also the truth about Emmet. And Wyldstyle. And Metal Beard. And Princess Unikitty.

And you.

Guess Who Said It First:
THE THINGS WE SAY THAT YOU NEVER KNEW WERE
from the Bible

▶ If Cinderella and Snow White ever spent days dreaming of being able to "eat, drink, and be merry" in the nearby castle, they wouldn't have been the first royalty to think that was the dream. King Solomon once had a misguided view of happiness also.

"A man hath no better thing under the sun, than to eat, and to drink, and to be merry: for that shall abide with him of his labour the days of his life, which God giveth him under the sun." (Eccl. 8:15 KJV)

RAPUNZEL: HEIR TO THE KING

In 1937 the world was introduced to the first Disney princess—Snow White. And ever since, toy stores have had difficulty keeping in stock tiaras, glass slippers, and ball gowns made to fit little girls four feet tall. For after Snow White, a multitude of other princesses followed, including Cinderella, Aurora, Belle, Ariel, Tiana, and most recently Anna and Elsa. And with each one came books, dolls, sticker albums, gowns, wands, jewelry, DVDs, CDs, new attractions at Disney World. . . . It's all so overwhelming, yet every little girl thinks she must have it all!

Each of the princesses has her own different story of how she had become or would later become a princess. Cinderella escaped her peasant life and fell in love with the prince in the nearby castle. Belle fell in love with a beast who ended up being a prince. Anna, Elsa, and Ariel were all born into royalty and lived their entire lives as such. But one, Rapunzel, has a story that may be unique when compared to the other princesses but is all too common when compared to the rest of the world.

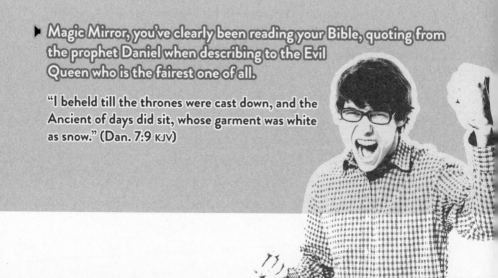

▶ Magic Mirror, you've clearly been reading your Bible, quoting from the prophet Daniel when describing to the Evil Queen who is the fairest one of all.

"I beheld till the thrones were cast down, and the Ancient of days did sit, whose garment was white as snow." (Dan. 7:9 KJV)

THAT'S Odd!

In the King James Version of the Bible, the word **king** can be found 1,756 times, **prince** is found 99 times, queen is found 52 times, but **princess** is found only once . . . and refers to a city . . . and in newer Bible translations has been changed to **queen**.

In the film *Tangled*, Rapunzel lives secluded high in a tower, never allowed to leave and only visited by the witch Gothel, whom she believes to be her mother. Gothel tells Rapunzel that the "outside world is a dangerous place filled with horrible, selfish people,"[21] which Rapunzel accepts as truth, never considering her "mother" would be lying to her. Yet at the same time she can't help but wonder about the lanterns in the sky that appear far away every year on her birthday. What exactly are they? Who is releasing them? Could they somehow be for her?

One day a fugitive named Flynn Rider with smoldering eyes and perfectly coifed hair climbs up Rapunzel's tower and promises to take her to go see the lanterns. And off they go on an adventure that will lead Rapunzel to a great deal more than just a few timely show tunes and a closer view of the lanterns. For she would learn the truth that Gothel had kept from her all of her life: Rapunzel was a lost child of a king.

Like the orphans in *Despicable Me*, we, too, have been adopted, except our Father is God the Creator. And similar to what the Croods learned, as God's children we are to no longer live in darkness but only in the light. As Emmet in *The LEGO Movie* needed to know his identity in order to live his life to the fullest, so must we know all the titles we are given when we become part of God's family. And perhaps the most important title of all given to us at our adoption is one that Rapunzel finally learned belonged to her: "heir."

> If we are God's children, that means we are His heirs along with the Anointed, set to inherit everything that is His.
> —Romans 8:17

> Since you belong to Him *and are now subject to His power,* you are the descendant of Abraham and the heir *of God's glory* according to the promise.
> —Galatians 3:29

> Now you are no longer a slave but God's own child. And since you are his child, God has made you his heir.
> —Galatians 4:7 NLT

"The Anointed" in Romans 8:17 above refers to Jesus, about whom Revelation 19:16 says, "And there on His robe and on His thigh was written His name: King of kings and Lord of lords." When we become children of God, we also become heirs to his kingdom, along with his Son, the King of kings. And like Gothel, who for her own selfish purposes could never tell Rapunzel who she truly was, so Satan never wants us to know the power we have in Jesus and the future secured for us in his kingdom despite our failings here on earth.

Upon Rapunzel's learning her true identity as child and heir to the king, Gothel's downfall began, leading to a fatal fall off of the tower she had imprisoned Rapunzel in her entire life—a fall not too different from Satan's fate: "Then I saw an angel coming down from heaven with the key to the bottomless pit and a heavy chain in his hand. He seized the dragon—that old serpent, who is the devil, Satan—and bound him in chains for a thousand years. The angel threw him into the bottomless pit, which he then shut and locked so Satan could not deceive the nations anymore" (Rev. 20:1–3 NLT).

Make no mistake about it—Satan is very aware of the fate God has already determined for him. But do all of God's children know the one awaiting them? Where they, as co-heirs with Jesus Christ the King of kings, are set to inherit what the apostle John could barely attempt to describe for us:

As I waited for what I thought was a bride, he showed me the holy city, Jerusalem, descending out of heaven from God. It gleamed *and shined* with the
glory of God; its radiance was like the most precious of jewels, like jasper, and
it was as clear as crystal. . . . The wall was made of jasper, while the city itself
was made of pure gold, yet it was as clear as glass. The foundation stones of
the wall of the city were decorated with every kind of jewel. . . .

And in the city, there is no need for the sun to light *the day* or moon *the
night* because the resplendent glory of the Lord provides the city with *warm,
beautiful* light and the Lamb illumines every corner *of the new Jerusalem.* And
all peoples of all the nations will walk by its *unfailing* light, and the rulers of
the earth will stream into the city bringing with them the symbols of their
grandeur and power. During the day, its gates will not be closed; the darkness of night will never settle in. The glory and grandeur of the nations will
be *on display there,* carried to the holy city by people *from every corner of the
world.* Nothing that defiles or is defiled can enter into its *glorious gates.* (Rev.
21:10–11, 18–19, 23–27)

Behind the Spells:
A REAL-LIFE WITCH

When King Saul became frightened after seeing the vast Philistine army, he
called out to God for help, but the Lord refused to answer him. So he did the
obvious next best thing . . . he set out to find a witch who could let him speak
to the dead prophet Samuel. Um . . . okay, Saul. He and his aides found a witch
in the town of Endor (not to be confused with the moon of Endor that the
Ewoks live on), who actually made contact with Samuel! Samuel's first words
to Saul were (obviously), "Why have you disturbed me?" Samuel goes on to
give Saul more bad news about how the battle will go the next day, and basically tells him at the end, "See you tomorrow" (wink, wink). Not wanting her
guest to leave on a bad note, the witch killed a calf, cooked up a feast, and fed
Saul and his men. (Talk about fattening up for the slaughter!) Read the story
for yourself in 1 Samuel 28.

IN **CONCLUSION**: GOD'S PURSUIT OF US WILL **NEVER CONCLUDE**

Emmet's favorite song is exactly right. Everything, indeed, is awesome, when a child of God lives each day knowing who he is in Christ, who he has in his corner, and the fate that lies ahead of him despite the troubles of today. Even in death, Vitruvius, the one who made up the prophecy concerning Emmet, did not stop believing that Emmet was still special and extraordinary, returning from the dead to tell him so.

Grug, the father of the Crood family, refused to let his family give up on living in the light. When the world was literally crumbling around them and the chasm between life in the caves and life in the light was growing wider, the powerful father threw each of his family members across toward the light. "No more caves!" he tells them as he sacrificially strands himself in the dark so that they could live in the light.[22]

When the evil Vector kidnaps Gru's newly adopted girls, young Agnes tells him, "He is gonna kick your butt,"[23] and then Gru proves her right as he dodges missiles, punches sharks, and strands Vector on the moon. "Margo, I will catch you," he tells the oldest sister at one point when she is scared to jump from danger into his arms. "And I will never let you go again!"[24] Nothing will separate Gru from his children any longer.

And Rapunzel's parents never stopped searching for their child either. Every year on her birthday, they would release the lanterns hoping she would see them and know they were for her. And when the prodigal child finally returned to them, the whole kingdom threw a party that lasted for a week, not unlike the party the father in Jesus' parable of the lost son threw for him upon his return: "Let's have a feast and celebrate," he told everyone, "because my son was dead and is alive again. He was lost and has been found" (Luke 15:23–24).

Yes, everything is awesome, when we know our Father in heaven will never give up on us either.

CHAPTER 4

NOW *I See It*, NOW I DON'T

In the comedy *Me, Myself & Irene*, Jim Carrey plays nice-guy Charlie Baileygates whom any woman would be proud to take home and introduce to her family. For eighteen years he has helped keep the state of Rhode Island safe by faithfully serving as a state trooper, and for almost just as long he has raised three boys who are not even his after their mother cheated on him and deserted them all for another man.

One problem, though: Charlie also suffers from something described in the movie as "advanced delusionary schizophrenia with involuntary narcissistic rage," which is basically a multiple personality disorder that causes him to turn into a foul-mouthed jerk named Hank Evans who takes it upon himself to get revenge on those who have done Charlie wrong.

Charlie is assigned to escort Irene Waters, played by Renée Zellweger, on a road trip to help keep her safe, and during this time Irene has to deal with both Charlie and Hank, oftentimes unsure who she's with and how to deal with him.

The unchurched audience today might be able to relate well with Irene, for the portrayals of Christians and Christianity in Hollywood has become much like someone suffering from multiple personality disorder or extreme bipolar tendencies. One moment actor Dennis Quaid is portraying an over-protective Christian parent who uses his influential role as pastor to ban all forms of dancing in his town; the next he is playing the cool, supportive surfer dad who sings "Blessed Be the Name of the Lord" at his church on the beach and doesn't get mad at his daughter when she sneaks out late to go to a beach party (*Footloose* and *Soul Surfer*, respectively). To the viewer who gets most of his opinions on Christianity from film and television, what is he supposed to take from these somewhat opposing views of what a Christian looks like?

From the Christians portrayed respectfully as on Joss Whedon's *Firefly*, to the cartoonishly awful stereotypes shown in movies such as *Saved!* and *Beautiful Creatures*, perhaps there is nothing in Hollywood more inconsistent than Christians and the faith they represent. What is the Christian faith about, and what do the majority of its followers truly believe? Let's sort through the good, the bad, and the ugly of Hollywood to try piecing it together.

 MINDY'S **COOL CHRISTIAN** BOYFRIEND

Name:

- Pastor Casey

Featured on:

- FOX sitcom *The Mindy Project*, introduced in season 1 episode "My Cool Christian Boyfriend"

Occupation:

- Lutheran pastor . . . then DJ . . . then event planner . . . then shoe salesman

Christian beliefs/practices:

- Thinks heaven will be strumming harps and playing doubles tennis with Abraham Lincoln and Tupac.

- Is not concerned with anyone's heart and what their beliefs are. Christianity is more like a club to join—take it or leave it, no big deal to him.

- Converting his Hindu girlfriend becomes no longer important to him.

- Not only is sex outside of marriage okay, but so are meaningless hook-ups with girls he just met.

- Goes to Haiti for a year to tell them about Jesus during the day . . . while sleeping with his non-Christian girlfriend at night.

- Believes pastors "are paid in the afterlife" and will live with their wives in a heavenly "McMansion."[1]

- Becomes convinced that God has called him to leave the ministry to become a DJ. (Okay, that one may be right. I don't think I would want this guy speaking on my behalf any longer either.)

Can oftentimes be seen:

- Singing Bruno Mars during a sermon.

- Being introduced in his church by Moby.

Best line:

- "Do you have any idea how hard it was for me to get these kids interested in Christianity? I had to tell them the apostles were the original One Direction, and they barely bought it."[2]

THE GOOD

Who says Christians can't be cool and well liked among the community? Being current with pop artists like Bruno Mars and One Direction is simply taking an interest in the culture of a Christian's mission field. And dressing in the latest fashions is almost human nature; of course Christians will also shop at the same stores as the rest of the world. The too-often-seen stereotype of churchgoers wearing nothing but cardigans and ankle-length denim skirts is not accurate for most of the church today. On the outside, Casey blends in with his mission field, as all believers are called to do so (1 Cor. 9:19–23).

From the first time Casey is introduced on the show, it is clear he has a heart for the people of Haiti, presumably in the wake of the 2010 earthquake that destroyed its capital, Port-au-Prince, and killed more than two hundred thousand people. When "My Cool Christian Boyfriend" aired in April 2013, it had been more than three years since the 7.0 earthquake took its toll on the third-world country. After such a long time, it is easy to forget about the great need for outsiders' help in Haiti, especially from the church, but Casey is still committed to sending food and supplies, as well as himself when he commits to moving there for a year. In his commitment to exchanging his comfortable New York lifestyle for a tent in Haiti for such a long time, he is remembering Jesus' statement to his disciples that "whatever you did to the least of these, so you did to Me" (Matt. 25:40).

THE BAD AND UGLY

The love Casey shows for the Haitians, however, does not match how he shows love to his Hindu girlfriend Mindy. In John 14:6, Jesus said, "I am the way and the truth and the life. No one comes to the Father except through me" (NIV). But this core belief of Christianity seems to be lost on Casey, for when Mindy expresses interest in his faith, Casey decides that he doesn't want her to convert but to stay true to who she is. His lack of concern for her disbelief in Jesus, combined with his apparent belief that the two of them will share a "McMansion" in heaven, implies a universalistic belief popular among many today that all (or at least multiple) roads lead to heaven. But Jesus said he was "*the* way," not "*a* way." Mindy's cool hipster Christian boyfriend may not like his faith being all about Jesus, but that's not up to him to decide.

Casey also has no internal conflict whatsoever concerning his sexual relationship with Mindy. But if he opened up the Bible he carried with him as he danced to Moby's walk-up song for him, he would find such scriptures as:

- Hold marriage in high esteem, all of you, and keep the marriage bed pure because God will judge those who commit sexual sins. (Heb. 13:4)

- Sexual immorality is a sin against your own body. . . . You have been purchased at a great price, so use your body to bring glory to God! (1 Cor. 6:18, 20)

- Each man should feel free to join together in sexual intimacy **with his own wife**, and each woman should join **with her own husband**. (1 Cor. 7:2, emphasis added)

Other Christian characters in Hollywood, such as Dr. April Kepner from *Grey's Anatomy*, have at least struggled with their belief in sexual abstinence outside of marriage before giving in to temptation, but not Casey. His relationship with Mindy, as well as his comments about one-night stands, shows a lack of concern for Scripture and for maintaining his body as a temple of the Holy Spirit (1 Cor. 6:19–20).

SHELDON'S **CRAZY CREATIONIST** MOM

Name:

- Mary Cooper, mother of physicist Sheldon Cooper

Featured on:

- CBS sitcom *The Big Bang Theory*, introduced in season 1 episode "The Luminous Fish Effect"

Place of residence:

- West Texas, which apparently is filled only with Southern-talking, church-going, gun-toting Bible thumpers

Can oftentimes be seen:

- Unknowingly making offensive racial comments toward many minority groups, with a focus on Asians
- Frowning upon her son's friends who have sexual relationships outside of marriage while she ends up "fornicating" herself, as Sheldon puts it
- Calling Catholics "rosary rattlers"

Best line:

- (to Raj the Hindu) "I made chicken. I hope that isn't one of the animals that you people think is magic."[3]

THE GOOD

Mary Cooper, the Bible-thumping mother of a stubborn, selfish evolutionist, clearly commands and has earned her son's total respect and love. There is no one Sheldon loves more than his mom, and his greatest fear is that she will be disappointed in him. Whatever she says he does, even now well into adulthood, in obedience to Paul's admonition in Colossians 3:20: "Children, always obey your parents, for this pleases the Lord" (NLT). And when there are problems to work through, Sheldon's friends know they can turn to her for guidance and to help get her son back on the right path. Despite the differences in their theological beliefs, Mary still holds the respect of the younger generation.

Sheldon's mother is also very open about her faith and does not compromise her beliefs, even when she leaves the comforts of home and visits mission fields, like what she calls "Gomorrah, California." She always insists on saying the blessing, even getting Sheldon and his group of nonbelieving friends involved; and when the entire group visits a popular tourist church in California, Mary gets them all to pray a short prayer aloud to God. Of course, most of her comments in showing her faith are used for comic relief (such as when she tells Jewish astronaut Howard that if he ever wants to live in the heavens for eternity, she's got a good book he can read), but the fact is, she doesn't back down from her faith or lean toward universalism in any way.

THE BAD AND UGLY

Most of the negative concerning Mary Cooper revolves around her silly and sometimes racially insensitive comments that are purely for laughs, such as:

- "Now after a moment of silent meditation, I'm gonna end with 'In Jesus' name.' But you two don't feel any obligation to join in . . . unless of course the Holy Spirit moves you."[4]

- "I can't spend twelve hundred dollars on a handbag, but it's free to look upon those who do with righteous condemnation."[5]

- "At our church we have a woman who's an amazing healer—mostly she does crutch and wheelchair people—but I'd bet she'd be willing to take a shot at whatever third-world demon is running around inside of you."[6]

And hopefully most can find the humor in jokes like these and understand the source material for what it is—a sitcom shooting for laughs. But it's important to point out here that a Christian has a responsibility to control their tongue, something James called "a spring of restless evil, brimming with toxic poisons." He continued, saying, "*Ironically* this same tongue can be *both an instrument* of blessing to our Lord and Father and *a weapon* that hurls curses upon others who are created in God's own image. One mouth streams forth both blessings and curses. My brothers and sisters, this is not how it should be" (James 3:8–10).

When Mary Cooper makes a comment about Raj's Hinduism or about the thin Asian-looking eyes she carves into the smiley face on Sheldon's grilled cheese, it's usually one that the apostle Paul would say about: "Don't let even one rotten word seep out of your mouths. Instead, offer only fresh words that build others up when they need it most. That way your good words will communicate grace to those who hear them" (Eph. 4:29). She would be wise to respect the power of the poisonous tongue and to remember to speak the truth in love (Eph. 4:15), especially when around Sheldon and his friends who are making internal decisions about her faith based on her words.

But of course, that's not nearly as funny as lines like "The Lord never gives us more than we can handle. Thankfully, he blessed me with two other children who were dumb as soup."[7]

THE MORAL COMPASS OF *SERENITY*

Name:

- Shepherd Book

Featured on:

- The 2002 cult hit TV show *Firefly* and the 2005 follow-up film *Serenity*

Can oftentimes be seen:

- Telling jokes and playing games with crew members who don't share his faith
- Reading his Bible during both times of rest and times of peril
- Fleeing temptation when among prostitutes but still defending them with his life
- Taking up arms to rescue his atheist captain
- Leading the crew in a time of prayer at mealtime
- Teaching a skeptic about faith

Best line:

- "If you take sexual advantage of her, you're going to burn in a very special level of hell. A level they reserve for child molesters and people who talk at the theater."[8]

THE GOOD

There's so much good to be found in this spaceship-traveling preacher brought to us by Joss Whedon, the creator of TV shows *Buffy the Vampire Slayer*, *Angel*, and *Dollhouse*, as well as the director of *The Avengers*. For a brief time in the fall of 2002, Whedon gave us perhaps one of the more admired and relatable Christian characters in recent television history.

Shepherd Book makes it clear from the beginning that he holds to a belief in a higher authority, and that this faith shapes the decisions he makes and how he lives his life. He tells the rest of the crew, "I believe there's a power greater than men—a power that heals."[9] He is often seen reading his Bible in the common areas and offering up biblically based advice to others.

Though the rest of the crew does not share Shepherd Book's beliefs, he gains their total respect by the way he loves them and risks his life for theirs. When a crew member asks him about the Bible having specific things to say about killing others, Book says, "Quite specific. It is, however, somewhat fuzzier on the subject of kneecaps."[10] And then the preacher goes out and actually shoots someone in the kneecaps while helping the crew rescue its captain.

But the greatest characteristic about Book concerns not necessarily him but the crew he made his home with onboard the ship *Serenity*, including:

- **Malcolm Reynolds:** A war veteran who lost his faith in God when his platoon wasn't saved in the war against the Alliance. "If I'm your mission," he tells Book, "best give it up. You're welcome on my boat. God ain't."[11]

- **Jayne Cobb:** An uneducated thief and mercenary who looks out only for himself, never hesitating to turn on someone if it means profit for him. The best thing he ever did was accidentally dump off of his escape ship a payload he stole, which inadvertently went to the poor townspeople he was leaving behind.

- **Inara Serra:** A companion, otherwise known as a high-end prostitute, who schedules "dates" on most every planet and moon they visit.

🗨 **Simon and River Tam:** A young man and his younger sister on the run from the authorities after breaking River out of Alliance control. For most of the show, River clearly has mental issues and is quite dangerous at times.

Along with a few others, we then have Shepherd Book, a pastor on mission and traveling away from his abbey for the first time in a while.

Which of these doesn't seem to belong with the others?

Yet Book lifts weights with the thief and betrayer, brings dinner to the prostitute, and plays cards and basketball with everyone. He simply becomes one of the crew. So much so that everyone risks their lives in order to get him help at an enemy hospital when he is near death.

"POP" QUIZ

1. Based on the company Shepherd Book keeps, is he more like:
  a. Jesus?
  b. Other Christians?
  c. Both A and B?
  d. Neither?

Answer: (a) Although it should be (c)

Skeptics, prostitutes, thieves . . . reminds me a lot of who Jesus found himself drawn to throughout his life on earth.

Jesus invited a thieving tax collector to be one of his disciples (Luke 5:27). He ate meals with what the religious leaders of that time called "immoral people" (Luke 5:30). He befriended a woman who had divorced five times and was currently living with a man who wasn't her husband (John 4:1–26), and then saved an adulteress from being stoned in accordance to the law (John 8:1–11). While never compromising who he was or allowing others to believe their sins were anything less than exactly what they were, Jesus befriended and loved the world, just as Shepherd Book did his best to do amongst the mixed crowd he found himself with.

THE BAD AND UGLY

Really, the only concern about Shepherd Book representing Christians is his sometimes-questionable theology. When River calls him out on the realism of Noah's ark ("We'll have to call it early quantum state phenomenon. Only way to fit five thousand species of animals on the same boat."[12]), Book's response that it doesn't have to make sense may seem to hint at a liberalism theology that believes many stories in the Bible were either altered or made up in order to teach a principle, but are not necessarily historically accurate. If this approach to the stories of the Bible is something Book agrees with, I would want to ask him how one can decide that stories like Noah's ark and Jonah are fictional or exaggerated but that young David truly did take down a giant with a sling shot. The books of the Bible in which stories such as these are found (i.e., Genesis and Exodus) were intended to be considered historical, not books filled with poetry and metaphors (i.e., Job and Revelation).

Book's dying words to Mal the skeptic ("I don't care what you believe. Just believe."[13]) were not representative of someone who had dedicated the last year of his life to loving this gang of misfits as Jesus loves them. The universalistic belief being implied here—that all faiths lead to the same ending, so just find one to dedicate your life to—does not match in any way what Book's Savior, Jesus, said while here on earth, and I would direct him to the same John 14:6 passage that Mindy's cool Christian boyfriend in *The Mindy Project* needs to read again. One's salvation must come through Jesus; he made no allowance for anything else. Would Book be happy if his friend Mal "just believed" that the afterlife were held deep in the abyss of the ocean and all its inhabitants worshiped an energetic sea sponge wearing square pants and living in a pineapple? I seriously doubt it. It's not the fact that we believe that matters; it's who or what we believe in.

BARNEY STINSON AND SHELDON COOPER AS POSITIVE BIBLICAL EXAMPLES

In the television shows mentioned above—*The Mindy Project*, *The Big Bang Theory*, and *Serenity*—as well as in many others such as *How I Met Your Mother*, *Cougar Town*, and '90s favorites *Friends* and *Seinfeld*, there is a common theme found among the group of friends that is worthy of our attention in a chapter that looks at what represents well both Christians and their faith. The group of friends, colleagues, or crew members their shows are centered around has chosen to live life together and build up and encourage one another, just as the first-century Christians did and as the Bible commands believers even today to do.

When the cul-de-sac crew in *Cougar Town* provides financial support, food, and a bed to sleep on to down-on-his-luck Bobby, they replicate well the picture the Christians in Acts gave us at the birth of the church: "There was an intense sense of togetherness among all who believed; they shared all their material possessions in trust" (Acts 2:44).

Time after time, the friends in *How I Met Your Mother* lived out Paul's admonition in 1 Thessalonians 5:14 to "encourage the downcast, to help the *sick and* weak, and to be patient with all of them" as they constantly nursed one another out of the broken-heart doldrums.

Penny and the gang of scientists in *The Big Bang Theory* seem to have dinner together every night in Leonard and Sheldon's apartment, according to the weekly menu Sheldon adheres to religiously (i.e., Monday is *always* Thai food night—never, ever pizza, Chinese, or some other food reserved for its own night). In doing so, they look a great deal like the first Christians, who "broke bread and shared meals with glad and generous hearts" (Acts 2:46).

Jesus' first disciples knew from the beginning the importance of their simply being together, even in times of fear and doubt (John 20:19; 21:1–3). New Testament writers would later say in their letters to other believers:

> Let us consider how to inspire each other to greater love and to righteous deeds, not forgetting to gather as a community, as some have forgotten, but encouraging each other, especially as the day *of His return* approaches. (Heb. 10:24–25)

> So support one another. Keep building each other up as you have been doing. (1 Thess. 5:11)

> Keep rejoicing and repair whatever is broken. Encourage each other, think as one, and live at peace. (2 Cor. 13:11)

When we see a group of friends on television living life together, eating meals with one another, spending hours at a time in a pub or coffee shop, and going above and beyond in the way they serve one another and encourage the brokenhearted, they are exemplifying the way Jesus intended his church to live out their lives, "especially as the day *of His return* approaches," as the Hebrews passage says above.

With the church being swept up in the same everyday routines and burdens as the rest of the world (i.e., school, work, sports, chores, kids' activities) that cause so many to introvert their lives because they barely have time to eat a meal with their family, let alone have coffee with a friend, is it possible that we can look to television to find the best examples around today of how God intended his body to live amongst each other?

Even Sheldon's mom might agree with that.

THE **CHRISTIAN** SCHOOL
STAFF AND STUDENTS FROM *SAVED!*

Names:

- Hilary Faye and Pastor Skip, specifically

Featured on:

- The 2004 Mandy Moore film *Saved!*

Can oftentimes be seen:

- Shooting guns at a shooting range called Emmanuel Shooting Range (with slogan "An eye for an eye")

- Doing flips on stage at a school assembly to "Whoomp! (There It Is)" and screaming, "Let's kick it Jesus-style!"[14]

- Telling kids in sex education classes that "it's all about populating the planet."[15]

- Passing out religious tracts instead of candy at Halloween

- In a loveless marriage (no wonder, since "it's all about populating the planet")

Best line:

- "I am *filled* with Christ's love!"[16] (said as she throws her Bible at someone she is trying to help)

THE GOOD

Unfortunately, most of the positives in this film come from the students who do not consider themselves Christians. But they are still worthy of pointing out as examples for how believers are called to live, and most in fact do. The film centers around a student, Mary, who gets pregnant but hides her secret out of fear for how her school will react if they find out. Two students, however—the Jewish "exile" Cassandra and the self-proclaimed non-Christian Roland—learn of Mary's secret and support her throughout, even helping her buy the right kinds of clothes that will hide her baby bump. The three of them form a strong friendship around Mary's crisis that never turns judgmental or condemning.

In the end, Mary ends up finding support from many of the people she feared would condemn her, including the dean of her school. The hodgepodge of a crowd visiting her and the baby in the hospital is a great picture of how people with different backgrounds and beliefs can come together at a crisis and find common ground amongst one another. Perhaps the Christians in the story will remember they are far from perfect also, and that as Paul says in Ephesians 2:8–9, they didn't earn God's grace, so they shouldn't go around bragging that they did something amazing. And maybe the outsiders will begin to see God's love through his children and one day allow God's grace to change their lives for eternity as well.

THE BAD AND UGLY

Though it is certainly possible that many of the stereotypes and characterizations of the Christians in *Saved!* were based on a miniscule percentage amount of Christians the makers of this film had seen in their lives, they have been heavily exaggerated for humor purposes.

In one amusing scene, Pastor Skip is teaching a sex ed class with pictures of a man and woman missing genitalia, and tells the class, "So, it's all about populating the planet, and good Christians don't get jiggy with it until they're married."[17] First, the Bible is clear that God created the incredible act of sex for our enjoyment as well as its functional purpose. A quick glance through the Song of Solomon while searching for the word *gazelle* reminds us how David's son King Solomon enjoyed his wife, and she him, and then God added this song to the biblical canon for us to read thousands of years later.

Second, Pastor Skip's reference that one can be a "good" Christian counters Jesus' statement to the rich young ruler that "No one is good—except God

> A quick glance through the Song of Solomon while searching for the word *gazelle* reminds us how David's son King Solomon enjoyed his wife, and she him.

alone" (Mark 10:18 NIV). The apostle Paul would later write to the church in Rome that "All have turned away; together they've become worthless. No one does good, not even one" (Rom. 3:12). So this "good Christian" Pastor Skip refers to is nonexistent, and it is an unfair level to set for anyone, let alone a group of impressionable students looking to him for guidance.

As discussed earlier when writing about Mindy's cool Christian boyfriend, the Scriptures are clear on God's intentions for sex staying within the covenant of marriage; but when characters like Pastor Skip elevate a specific sin (in this case, premarital sex) above others and label those who abstain from that one but perhaps not others as still "good," this is not accurate in the least of God's view toward that person or sin. First John 3:4 says that "all sin is contrary to the law of God" (NLT), meaning that the one who abstains from premarital sex but gossips about those who do not is just as guilty in the eyes of God as the one he or she feels superior over. However, Jesus assured us that "all sin and blasphemy can be forgiven" (Mark 3:28 NLT) and was done so by his sacrifice on the cross.

> This idea of Christian superiority and refusing to relate with the rest of the world is not something someone would learn from reading the Bible.

The general viewpoint of all the so-called Christians in Saved! is that the world needs to come to them and adapt to their culture, instead of the other way around, which would involve Christians immersing themselves in the surrounding culture and getting to know the needs of their mission field in order to best lead others to a relationship with Jesus. This is shown in their "holier than thou" attitude toward outsiders and in their distributing every kid's least favorite Halloween goodie—a religious tract. They scream at and picket against those on the other side of controversial issues and disown Cassandra because of her Jewish beliefs, instead of loving everyone as Jesus loves them.

This idea of Christian superiority and refusing to relate with the rest of the world is not something someone would learn from reading the Bible. Paul, the first missionary, taught us long ago just how much Christians should submerge themselves into their mission field:

> I have become a slave *by my own free will* to everyone *in hopes* that I would gather more *believers.* When around Jews, I emphasize my Jewishness in order to win them over. When around those who live *strictly* under the law, I live by its regulations—even though I have a different perspective on the law now—in order to win them over. *In the same way,* I've made a life outside the law to gather those who live outside the law (although I personally abide by and live under the Anointed One's law). I've been *broken, lost, depressed, oppressed, and* weak that I might *find favor and* gain the weak. I'm *flexible, adaptable, and* able to do and be whatever is needed for all kinds of people so that *in the end* I can use every means at my disposal to offer them salvation. I do it all for the gospel *and for the hope* that I may participate with everyone who is blessed by the proclamation of the good news. (1 Cor. 9:19–23)

Paul "made a life outside the law to gather those who live outside the law" and became "*flexible, adaptable, and* able to do and be whatever is needed for all kinds of people." In other words, he went to them as they were and found a way to love and reach them, a far cry from the evangelism efforts of the Christians in *Saved!*

Guess Who Said It First:
THE THINGS WE SAY THAT YOU NEVER KNEW WERE *from the Bible*

▸ To Hilary Faye and friends from *Saved!* who consider themselves "holier than thou," please see what God's people said about themselves in Isaiah 65 and consider it fair warning. [Note: It didn't end well for them.]

"Stand by thyself, come not near to me; for I am holier than thou." (Isa. 65:5 KJV)

▶ Though Mary Cooper could certainly not be called a false prophet, when she told her son it was very Christian of him to condemn her internally while appearing to accept her, she might still be insinuating living as a "wolf in sheep's clothing," something Jesus spoke of long ago.

"Beware of false prophets, which come to you in sheep's clothing, but inwardly they are ravening wolves." (Matt. 7:15 KJV)

⬇ **TOO MANY** TO DETAIL

The previously mentioned multifarious Christians from *Footloose* and *Soul Surfer*, both played by the same actor. The highly questionable Christians in the young teen novel series and movie *Beautiful Creatures* who pray aloud against a classmate, screaming crazily, "Please, Jesus help me!"[18] The stick-in-the-mud Angela from *The Office* who said the only two books she would bring with her if she were stranded on a deserted island would be the Bible and *The Purpose Driven Life*, but then has sexual relationships with multiple men at the same time. The iconic, always-loveable Ned Flanders from *The Simpsons*, with such memorable quotes as, "I'm not thinking straight, why did I have that wine cooler last month?"[19] "Whoa, a Methuselah rookie card!"[20] and "Dear neighbor, you are my brother. I love you, and yet I feel a great sadness in my bosom."[21]

The Christianity we see on television and in the movies has more personalities than *Survivor All-Stars*. And not even mentioned in this chapter are the countless roles of priests in demonic films ranging from *The Exorcism of Emily Rose* to *Insidious*, or the Catholic faiths found on one side of the spectrum in the CBS show *Blue Bloods* to the opposite side found within the families of mafia films. How can the unchurched possibly decipher what Christianity is from observing this array of fictional portrayals?

Jesus' audience once had a similar conundrum. With an astounding 613 laws given in the Old Testament, many were understandably unsure of what to focus on: "Teacher, which is the greatest commandment in the Law?" they asked him one day. He replied, "'Love the Lord your God with all your heart and with all your soul and with all your mind.' This is the first and greatest commandment. And the second is like it: 'Love your neighbor as yourself.' All the Law and the Prophets hang on these two commandments" (Matt. 22:36–40 NIV). And Paul would later tell the church in Galatia, "For the whole law comes down to this one instruction: 'Love your neighbor as yourself'" (Gal. 5:14).

To the Irene Waters of the world confused by the multiple personalities of Christians on the screen, maybe they should hold loving others as the litmus test for figuring out whether what is being portrayed is accurate. The term *Christian* literally means "little Christ." So if Jesus' main concern on this earth was loving others, then all the "little Christs" of this world, fictional and real, are most like their Savior when they love others as he loves them.

CHAPTER 5

I ONCE WAS *LOST* BUT *Now* I AM ...

Without Anything Good on Television

In 2004, Oceanic Airlines flight 815 crashed on a mysterious island. Over the next forty-five days, Dr. Jack Shephard became the anointed leader of the survivors, con man James "Sawyer" Ford struggled to live civilly amongst a community, convict Kate Austen became the apple of both their eyes, and paralyzed John Locke could suddenly walk again (which was a good thing, since everyone was running for their lives from a mysterious monster in the jungle). By the time the survivors discovered and blew up a door to an underground hatch and young Walt was kidnapped by the Others, the viewing audience was hooked—there was a new *it* show on television.

Lost's overwhelming popularity right from the start was the beginning of a resurgence toward the sci-fi mystery genre on television. Sure, there had been others before *Lost—The X-Files* comes to mind—but beginning in 2005, after the overwhelming success of *Lost's* first season, networks up and down the

The creators and writers of Lost reached our hearts by engaging mankind's need for redemption, forgiveness, and love.

satellite guide began filling up their new seasons with *Lost*-like copycat shows. No other shows about island castaways, of course, but aliens, the supernatural, and other phenomena abounded on new shows.

Less than only a decade later, this TV-show lover cannot recall a single one of them. There was something about an underwater alien or monster on NBC with a kid in it. . . . An ABC show that also had aliens in the water, called *Intruder*, or *Invisible*, or something like that. I could find out on IMDb.com, but why bother? Obviously it was no *Lost*.

Why did these other shows struggle to find the popularity that *Lost* had found? Weren't they targeted toward the same audiences? Didn't they fill their episodes with supernatural oddities and unexplainable mysteries, just as *Lost* did? Weren't their actresses attractive too? What was so special about Kate and Juliet?

The success of *Lost*, in large part, was not simply because of the engaging storylines. Nor was it only because it had the best-looking actors or the most jaw-dropping cliffhangers. The creators and writers of *Lost* reached our hearts by engaging mankind's need for redemption, forgiveness, and love. The storylines and plot twists revolved around this foundation, rather than the other way around, as was the case with many failed attempts to replicate the culture buzz that exploded with *Lost*.

Thousands of years ago, man's Creator decided the way he would most communicate to his people was through the written word of the Bible. This Book "is God-breathed; *in its* inspired *voice, we hear* useful teaching, rebuke, correction, *instruction, and* training for a life that is right" (2 Tim. 3:16). God intended its message of redemption, forgiveness, and love to reach every man and woman throughout time, on every continent, and in every culture. By building their show's foundation around the same eternal themes, the creative minds behind *Lost* also created a show that has the ability to break through cultural barriers and appeal to the masses throughout multiple generations.

Entire books could be written on *Lost* and all the faith and theology Easter eggs to be found in it; in fact, at least one thought-provoking one has.[1] In this chapter, however, are simply six of the top biblical metaphors/lessons/story-lines that stood out to me the most upon rewatching this show in research for this book. (Without a doubt, the best month of my life!)

EVERYONE HAS **A PENNY LOOKING** FOR THEM

***Lost's* first season** finale left audiences with one question to agonize over for the entire summer: What is in the hatch? The answer, as revealed in the season two premiere: a number-punching, jumpsuit-wearing, exercise bike–riding Scotsman named Desmond Hume. (Nobody won that office bet, I tell you.) As Desmond's storyline progressed when he returned to the beach at the end of the second season, we are introduced via flashbacks to the love of his life, Penny Widmore.

In the season three episode "Flashes Before Your Eyes," Desmond and Penny are madly in love, near engagement we soon find out, and Desmond meets with Penny's father, Charles Widmore, to ask him for Penny's hand in marriage. But Charles does not give the answer Desmond was expecting. "You will never be a great man," Charles tells him. "How could you ever be worthy of my daughter?"[2] The seed has now been planted inside Desmond: he does not deserve Penny.

A short time later, with an engagement ring in his pocket, Desmond gives in to the lie Charles fed him and ends his relationship with Penny. "You deserve someone better," he tells her. In which she responds, "I chose to be with you. I love you." But it's too late. There's no convincing Desmond otherwise. "Why do you love me?" he asks, but no answer from her will matter.[3] He is not worthy of Penny, he believes, and sets off on a journey to earn her love.

At an unspecified time later, Desmond decides the way he is going to prove that he deserves Penny is by winning a boat race around the world, a race that is sponsored by Charles Widmore himself. He is convinced he must earn back the love that Penny is willing to give him freely. And it is during this race around the world that he crashes on the island and finds himself punching a button every 108 minutes for three years.

And all for nothing, as Penny had never stopped loving him.

Desmond would undoubtedly agree with the apostle Paul's sentiment that "No one is righteous—not even one. . . . All have turned away; together they've become worthless. No one does good, not even one" (Rom. 3:10, 12). Why would Penny still love a "worthless" Desmond, he must have thought to himself all those days alone on the ocean and then the island. And why would God love Paul, a man responsible for killing many first-century Christians?

Perhaps the answer is found in who Paul was quoting in the Romans 3 passage: the psalmist. For the psalmist also sang to God such praises as, "For Your loyal love for me is so great *it is beyond comparison*. You have rescued my soul from the depths of the grave" (Ps. 86:13) and "Your love, O Eternal One, towers high into the heavens. Even the skies are lower than Your faithfulness" (36:5) and "For Your amazing mercy ascends far into the heavens; Your truth rises above the clouds" (57:10). Can anyone truly comprehend God's love for us, his creation? If King David, the writer of many of the psalms, someone God described as "a man after My own heart" (Acts 13:22), could not, then what hope do the rest of us have? Like Desmond, we are left asking, "Why do you love me?"

Because his love is just that amazing.

And there is nothing we can do to earn God's love, just as Desmond couldn't earn Penny's love for him with a boat race around the world. She gave it to him willingly. Long before he left on his journey.

But there was great news for Desmond, as we learn in the final scene from season two: Penny was looking for him. Like the prodigal son, Desmond was lost, but Penny was searching, keeping watch, waiting for him with open arms. She would find him if it was the last thing she did, as she told him in the classic

There is nothing we can do to earn God's love, just as Desmond couldn't earn Penny's love for him with a boat race around the world.

season four episode "The Constant" when they were able to speak briefly on a satellite phone:

DESMOND: "You still care about me?"
PENNY: "I've been looking for you for the past three years."
DESMOND: "I've always loved you. I'm so sorry."
PENNY: "I'll find you, Des, no matter what."[4]

That SOUNDS a LITTLE Like *Scripture*

Jacob to Hurley concerning "evil Locke": "He is certainly going to try to kill you."[5]

1 Peter 5:8: "Your enemy the devil is prowling around outside like a roaring lion, just waiting and hoping for the chance to devour someone."

Jacob to Jack, whom he was leaving in charge after he was gone: "Drink this."[6]

Matthew 26:27: "Take this and drink" (what Jesus said to his disciples, whom he was leaving in charge of his mission after he was gone).

Temple leader Dogen to Sayid, on instructing him how to kill "evil Locke": "If you allow him to speak, it is already too late."[7]

Ephesians 4:27: "Do not give the devil a foothold" (NIV).

Ben to Jack, when asked if the apostle Thomas was ever able to fully believe in the resurrected Christ: "Of course he was. We're all convinced sooner or later."[8]

Romans 14:11: "Every knee will bow down to Me. Every tongue will confess to God."

Jacob to Richard, when asked about his home in the base of the statue: "No one comes in unless I invite them in."[9]

John 6:44: "No one can come to me unless the Father who sent me draws them" (NIV).

"I am the good shepherd. The good shepherd lays down His life for the sheep *in His care*" (John 10:11).

316: THE **ONLY** WAY

Midway through season one, it becomes obvious to audiences that numbers mean a lot on this show. Even several years after the show has ended, I can recite the following numbers without hesitation if asked. All you other Losties, join me in chorus: 4, 8, 15, 16, 23, 42. And when you go back and watch old episodes, you see these numbers popping up in all kinds of ways; most obvious of course is the Oceanic flight number of the plane that crashed on the island: 815.

But three years later when the Oceanic Six (the castaways who found a way off of the island) desperately need to return to the island, they are told by the mysterious Eloise Hawking that they absolutely must take Ajira Airways flight 316 in order to get back. Flight 316? Wait a second. Okay, so there is a 16, but what about the 3? How come these numbers don't line up with Hurley's numbers the way everything else in the show has?

But the numbers 316 do have meaning, don't they? And much more so than just retired Yankees jersey numbers. (You can look it up if you want, but it's true. Not relevant, but true.) Perhaps the most powerful numbers in the Bible:

John 3:16—"For God so loved the world that he gave his one and only Son, that whoever believes in him shall not perish but have eternal life." (NIV)

When Eloise Hawking shows Jack a binder listing all the flights that would seemingly take them over the area where the island is, the binder is filled with pages listing hundreds of flights. But she is quite adamant about Ajira flight 316. "It *must* be that plane," she tells him.[10] Flight 316 was the only way back to the island.

Did I forget to mention that fellow castaway *John* Locke was the one put in charge of bringing the Oceanic Six back? *John* Locke. Flight *316*. Let's squeeze it together now . . . John 3:16. And then there was John's note that he wrote to Jack just before he died, revealed to us in season five episode "316": "I wish you had believed me."[11]

Yeah, numbers mean a lot in *Lost*. But the message of the episode "316" carries the most importance. There are many routes people take to try and find their way to God. Eloise Hawking could fill a binder full of pages listing all of them. But there is only one way that will work, and the answer is found in the numbers 316. John 3:16.

 JACK THE **SACRIFICIAL LAMB**

In the series finale, appropriately titled "The End," the island has become unplugged, so to speak, and one of the remaining survivors must go down into a cave and fix it. Whoever goes down there will not be coming up, meaning he will be sacrificing his life to literally save the entire world. (It's difficult to explain. There's something about a light, a cork, and a whole bunch of other things that went over my head. But long story short: the entire world would be destroyed if it wasn't corrected.)

Jack Shephard volunteers himself to be the world's savior, and he completes his mission heroically, dying as expected in the process.

But many stories have sacrificial figures in them, right? Jack Bauer from *24*, for one, is always willing to sacrifice his life for others (yet only his co-stars seem to die). But no one is attempting to compare America's favorite CTU agent to the Messiah, so what makes Jack Shephard so special?

I'm glad you asked.

First is our hero's name. The "e" in "shepherd" may have been changed to an "a," but the symbolism is still the same. In John 10:11, Jesus said, "I am the good shepherd. The good

> "I find it a little odd that your scripture stick has dried blood on it."[12]
>
> —Charlie, referring to Mr. Eko's stick that has been used as both a reminder of scripture and a weapon

shepherd lays down His life for the sheep *in His care*." And long before Jesus' birth, it was prophesied through Micah, "But you, Bethlehem of Ephrathah, . . . From your people will come a Ruler who will be the shepherd of My people" (Mic. 5:2). There is no shortage in Scripture of verses illustrating Jesus as a shepherd and us being his sheep needing to be saved by him.

Second, moments before Jack's descent into the cave, he is stabbed by "evil Locke" (a.k.a. the man in black) in the side. As the blood gushes from his side, it is pouring down rain, mixing the blood with the water. Does this feel a little déjà vu? A little familiar? Here's why: "One soldier took his spear and pierced [Jesus'] abdomen, which brought a gush of blood and water" (John 19:34).

It wasn't necessary to have Jack stabbed in the side. A deep plunge in his gut or back would've been just as effective. It also didn't have to be raining during this scene. In fact, the rain stopped completely just shortly after. But the comparison to Christ's sacrifice was being driven home.

Third, we have to return to those mysterious numbers. In the season six episode "The Substitute," we find the names of our plane crash survivors etched on the walls of a cave with numbers written next to them. Next to the name "Shephard"? The number 23. As in Psalm 23, "The LORD is my shepherd" (v. 1 NLT).

But there's more concerning the number 23. And if it's a coincidence, then it's a weird one. But it begins with recognizing that the book of Luke seems to have been sprinkled into the mythology of *Lost*. In another episode, Richard Alpert is seen reading Luke 4. (Four? As in 4, 8, 15 . . . ? Huh, that's odd.) Also, Jesus' famous trilogy of parables—the *lost* coin, the *lost* sheep, and the *lost* son, which has great meaning to all the lost souls in this show, both physically and otherwise—is found in Luke 15. (Wait—15? Come on, this can't be a coincidence!)

So what is found in Luke 23? The crucifixion and death of Jesus. The Shepherd sent to save the world, who was stabbed in the side, with blood and

> **It wasn't necessary to have Jack stabbed in the side. But the comparison to Christ's sacrifice was being driven home.**

water flowing from the wound. And without this sacrifice, the entire world would be lost.

 RICHARD ALPERT—THE **LOST DISCIPLE**

Richard Alpert arrived on the island in 1867 when the slave ship the *Black Rock* found itself in a typhoon and washed ashore. After going through his own version of Satan's temptation of Jesus he was reading about previously in Luke 4, he asks Jacob, the godlike figure of the island, to make him ageless, which Jacob does. He is then appointed as an advisor and Jacob's liaison to the Others, which he serves as faithfully for the next 140 years. But after Jacob is killed, something Richard didn't feel could ever happen, he pretty much freaks out. Knowing he is not able to end his own life due to being given his special gift from Jacob, he begs Jack to light the nearby dynamite for him so that he could finally leave this earth. When Jack questions his motives for doing such a thing, Richard explains,

> I devoted my life longer than you can possibly imagine in service of a man who told me that everything was happening for a reason, that he had a plan, a plan that I was a part of. And when the time was right, that he'd share it with me. And now that man's gone. So why do I want to die? Because I just found out that my entire life had no purpose.[13]

You won't find any quotes like this in Scripture, but that doesn't mean something very similar to this wasn't ever said before by one of our New Testament heroes, specifically the remaining disciples after Jesus' death, but before his resurrection.

Imagine being Peter or Thomas or Matthew. Three years previously, a man performing miracles said, "*Come*, follow Me, and I will make you fishers of men" (Matt. 4:19), and you packed up everything and did just that. You watched him feed thousands out of just a few fish, heal the sick by just his words, and even resurrect a friend who had been dead for days. This was undoubtedly the prophesied Messiah everyone had been waiting for, and he would soon take his rightful place as king on the throne of Jerusalem.

And then he dies. Without even a fight.

What would be going through your mind? What do you think was going through their minds? I think Richard's little rant to Jack right before he tries to blow himself up with dynamite sounds pretty dead-on to me. Scripture does tell us they were scared, just as Richard was: "On that same evening (Resurrection Sunday), the followers gathered together behind locked doors in fear" (John 20:19). I can see Matthew going on and on about how he had left his high-paying job as a tax collector to devote his life to Jesus' ministry. No doubt Peter had something to say about Jesus promising him he had a plan and that Peter was part of it. And feeling they had no purpose elsewhere, James and the other former fishermen went back to their old fishing holes they had left when they decided to follow Jesus.

> "Jesus Christ is not a weapon!"[14]
>
> —Hurley's mom upon finding him about to attack the supposed house intruders with a Jesus figurine.

But as we know, Jesus reappeared to the disciples and gave them their new mission: "Go out and make disciples in all the nations" (Matt. 28:19). Richard, too, found new purpose, a renewed mission, when Jack (our Savior figure, remember) sat right next to him as the fuse on the dynamite became shorter and shorter, with a faith that could move mountains (or in this case, put out a fuse without even touching it).

 ## A **GRACE** LIKE NONE OTHER

Any guess on what the three most powerful words in all of *Lost* were? Not "Look! A freighter!" Nor "Move the island," "Not Penny's boat," or "The smoke monster!" Rather, the three most powerful, life-changing, jaw-dropping words of *Lost* had to be "I'll have you."

Some context now would be helpful.

Half a book could be written on Benjamin Linus, perhaps the most disturbing, convoluted, and yet pitiable character on the show. In the limited space here, though, it may be best to just sum up his life in a pros and cons list:

CONS

- Killed his dad just before betraying the Dharma Initiative and helping the Others to lead a purge in wiping out the people he grew up with on the island

- Kidnapped a French woman's baby

- Raised said baby as his own daughter before allowing her to be killed right before his eyes

- Kidnapped pregnant Claire

- Lied to Juliet continually to keep her on the island with him

- Was indirectly responsible for the deaths of multiple castaways, most notably Ana Lucia and Libby

- Kidnapped Walt

- Killed John Locke (the real one)

- Killed Jacob

PROS

- Has some pretty good one-liners

Despite the uneven list above, Ben Linus is a character you can't help but root for, because you see the good in him being suppressed by his loyalty to the island. And when Ilana, who loved Jacob like a father, learns that Ben killed him, she forces Ben at gunpoint to dig his own grave. When he is finished, she plans on shooting him and burying him there. At a moment when her back is turned, he runs off into the jungle to grab a rifle that "evil Locke" has left for him there. Ilana chases him with her own firearm and when he picks up Locke's rifle, there is a standoff. But Ben has no intentions to shoot Ilana; he only wishes to explain himself:

BEN: I sacrificed everything for [Jacob]. And he didn't even care. Yeah, I stabbed him. I was . . . so angry . . . confused . . . I was terrified that I was about to lose the only thing that had ever mattered to me—my power. But the thing that really mattered was already gone. I'm sorry that I killed Jacob. I am, and I do not expect you to forgive me, because . . . I can never forgive myself.

ILANA: Then what do you want?

BEN: Just let me leave.

ILANA: Where will you go?

BEN: To Locke.

ILANA: Why?

BEN: Because he's the only one that'll have me.

ILANA: (long pause) I'll have you.[15]

The three most powerful words in all of *Lost*. Not because of who said them, or who they were said to. But because of what they represent: grace. God's grace. Given to us not because of who we are or what we did, but only because of who God is and what Jesus did.

Romans 6:23 tells us that "the wages of sin is death, but the gift of God is eternal life in Christ Jesus our Lord" (NIV). In other words, what we deserve (death), we don't get. What we don't deserve (eternal life in heaven), we get. And all from God, because of his Son, Jesus.

Grace is an unfathomable concept to a human race that lives and dies by the law, by giving out and receiving just rewards. To the world, bad deserves bad; good deserves good. (But how "good" can one really be?) Like the apostle Paul, the wisest among us believe we are "the worst of them all" (1 Tim. 1:15). How could anyone forgive us? How could anyone love us? Sacrifice his own Son for us? Welcome us into his kingdom?

"I'll have you," God says to us.

The look on Ben's face upon being extended Ilana's grace says it all. He doesn't understand. He can't wrap his mind around it. Did she forget already that he has done so many horrible things, including killing her father figure? How can she not only let him live but welcome him back into her camp?

That is God's grace. Unexplainable, yet real nevertheless.

IT'S Not ALL GOSPEL in *LOST*

In the season six episode "Ab Aeterno," Jacob tells Richard, "That man who sent you to kill me [the man in black] believes that every man is corruptible and that it's in their very nature to sin. I bring people here to prove him wrong. And when they get here, their past doesn't matter."[16]

Uh, sorry, Jacob. But I guess your brother, the man in black, has read the Bible a bit more than you, specifically the apostle Paul's letter to the Romans: "For I know that good itself does not dwell in me, that is, in my sinful nature. For I have the desire to do what is good, but I cannot carry it out" (Rom. 7:18 NIV). And you also may want to do a word search in the Bible for "corrupt." Yeah, we're all pretty corruptible. But, hey, you got the part about our past not mattering to God! Good for you. Now go point those puppy-dog eyes at someone else.

THE **REUNION** LIKE NO OTHER

You may have heard that the *Lost* finale didn't exactly go over like gangbusters. Not necessarily how the adventures on the island ended, but the mystery revealed to the secret of the final season's "flash-sideways." I will attempt not to ruin it for anyone I may have convinced with this chapter to go watch all six seasons of *Lost*, so let me just touch for a moment on something that none of us really knows will be like, certainly not the writers of a TV show: the reuniting with our loved ones in heaven. (Oh well, I think I just ruined it for you.)

Rewatching the finale ended up being much more of an emotional experience than I was expecting. But as Jin and Sun saw their baby on the monitor and began remembering, as Kate helped Claire deliver her baby and they both remembered everything, as Sawyer kissed Juliet and remembered, after all those years apart . . . wow! As amazing and emotional as that was, it was only TV. How much more awesome will it be to first lay our eyes on Jesus upon entering heaven? What will it be like when we see loved ones? Will we recognize each other right away? Will we know our parents as our parents and our kids as our kids? Whatever the answers may be, it will be a thrilling, goose bump–inducing moment. And though there are some major theological problems with the afterlife of *Lost*, I believe the emotional reunions are a much more accurate picture than playing baseball in *Field of Dreams*, rescuing loved ones from hell in *What Dreams May Come*, or avenging your death in *Ghost*.

In the final scene, when Jack realizes where he is and remembers everything, he opens up his dad's coffin, only to find it empty. But he finds his dad behind him alive and well. As will be the case in heaven, for the "dead will live, LORD; their bodies will rise—let those who dwell in the dust wake up and shout for joy" (Isa. 26:19 NIV). As Jack begins asking questions to his dad who died long ago, one of his first deals with the issue of time . . . when . . . now.

> How much more awesome will it be to first lay our eyes on Jesus upon entering heaven?

"There is no now . . . here," his dad affirms for Jack.[17] For there is no time in heaven. At least not with the restrictions it forces us to live under here on earth. Are there 24-hour days, 7-day weeks, 365-day years? I'm not sure. But it won't matter, for God has "set eternity in the human heart" (Eccl. 3:11 NIV), and though we cannot fathom a timeless existence now, we will one day.

Guess Who Said It First:
THE THINGS WE SAY THAT YOU NEVER KNEW WERE
from the Bible

▶ Hey, maybe Ben wasn't so bad after all. He was even quoting God when he told Sayid that he'll always be a killer, that a leopard cannot change his spots.

"Can the Ethiopian change his skin, or the leopard his spots?" (Jer. 13:23 KJV)

▶ Ageless Richard has heard it a thousand times: he's as old as the hills, just as Job was once asked by his buddy Eliphaz:

"Art thou the first man that was born? Or wast thou made before the hills?" (Job 15:7 KJV)

★ ★ ★

Lost was a show that made us think, ponder, and converse with others about the plots and characters—about general truths being told—that as believers we know to be Spirit-inspired. How "evil Locke" tempts others by lying to them about being able to give them what they most want. The season five finale that deals with free will, yet still under the sovereignty of the island. The tapestry that Jacob weaves throughout his time on the island. The redemption stories of Jack, Sawyer, Kate, Sayid, and others. The statue of Jesus with open arms in the church parking lot during the finale, when those from the island meet in the afterlife.

The show connected with the culture because it brought us biblical parallels that tapped into themes, ideas, and emotions that everyone deals with, struggles with, and is instilled with by their Creator. Who on this earth is not in need of redemption, grace, and forgiveness? Who would say they do not need a Penny searching for them, no matter the cost? Is there anyone who has ever lost a loved one who has not laid awake at night wondering if they would someday be reunited and what that would be like? Like Richard Alpert, we all struggle with purpose and are confused when life deals us a hand we did not see coming.

God communicates to us concerning these and so much more in his eternal Book. When a show such as *Lost* attempts to do the same, focusing on these elements as its foundation, the resulting success should not be surprising, since it is merely replicating the best-selling book of all time.[18]

CHAPTER 6

THE GOD of Reality

In 1992 MTV threw a handful of polarizing characters together in a house and followed them around with cameras, calling it *The Real World*. The modest success that MTV found among its younger viewers was worthy of notice for a cable network, enough so to warrant a seemingly unlimited amount of follow-up versions, all based in different cities around the world. But eight years after *The Real World*'s premiere, Richard Hatch paraded around naked on an island with host Jeff Probst and fifteen other contestants, and *Survivor* changed television history forever. The networks enjoyed the combination of ridiculous amounts of advertising dollars and low-budget productions, and the viewing public realized they loved to watch other people live their lives. Voyeurism became a win-win.

Talent competition shows like *American Idol* and *So You Think You Can Dance?* became all the talk in the office break rooms. *Fear Factor* and *The Amazing Race* got everyone and their mother applying online for their fifteen minutes of fame. Women everywhere dreamed of what it would be like to find their husband on *The Bachelor* and men got giddy over the idea of visiting *Temptation Island.* Self-obsessed celebrity wannabes got cameras to follow them around at both Laguna Beach and the Jersey Shore. Even celebrities got in on the action with shows like *Dancing with the Stars* and *Celebrity Apprentice.*

The kitchen chefs from hell, the hoarders, the home renovators, the socialites who will do anything to get out of having a real job, the Southerners who are apparently great fodder for the viewing audience . . . there is a reality show for everything nowadays. And today I say that is a good thing. For within these widely appealing forms of entertainment for the twenty-first century, we have—perhaps more so than in any fictional show—God's children living through "the day the Lord has made" for them (Ps. 118:24 NLT), and we get to see these days of theirs thanks to the camera crews and the producers count-ing their hundred-dollar bills.

And also, as has been the case with the previous discussions in this book, it is rather difficult to avoid all the themes and ideas found in God's eternal Bible, the greatest influencer of mankind in all of history. Maybe the producers of *Naked and Afraid* didn't have in mind Hebrews 4:13—"Nothing in all creation is hidden from God. Everything is naked and exposed before his eyes, and he is the one to whom we are accountable" (NLT)—when they came up with the premise of disrobing two strangers and dropping them off in the middle of nowhere for twenty-one days, but the comparison is there nonetheless. As is the case with many other hit reality shows worthy of our discussion.

 EVERYONE'S A **FIXER UPPER**

There's a strong chance that at any time during the day or night, one can turn on HGTV and find dust in the air and a hammer or skill saw in someone's hand. In recent years, the name of the game for what was originally called the Home, Lawn, and Garden Channel has become "home renovation," or more exactly, "televising home renovation." With an apparently endless supply of marathons for shows such as *Flip or Flop, Love It or List It, Property Brothers,* and *House Hunters Renovation,* women around the world dream up their family's next reno project every weekend as their husband snores in his La-Z-Boy.

God has taken on billions of fixer uppers throughout all of history, beginning with the first two—Adam and Eve—and continuing right on up to you and me.

One of the more recent HGTV renovation hits, *Fixer Upper*, debuted in 2014 and has set itself apart slightly from many of the network's other shows that feature homes costing well out of the average viewer's budget being renovated by former Abercrombie & Fitch models. The show features Chip and Joanna Gaines of Waco, Texas, who live on a farm with their four children (and cows and goats and whatever other animals Chip decides to bring home) and together run a realty/remodeling company called Magnolia Homes. The concept of their show is simple: they show three different houses to a family wanting to buy in the area—all three choices will be run-down homes desperately in need of some TLC—and they are given at least thirty thousand dollars to make the needed renovations for whichever home is chosen.

Oftentimes it is quite tough for the client to see Chip and Joanna's vision for the home. Most of the houses they walk into require major work on the flooring, walls, bathrooms, kitchen . . . pretty much everything. Fireplaces need to be ripped out, walls will be torn down—the herculean work ahead for all of them is daunting. But as to be expected, Chip and Joanna always pull through and blow the home owners' expectations out of the water with their almost-miraculous renovation.

The tagline for the show is "Do you have the guts to take on a fixer upper?" Because what Chip and Joanna already know is that their client will never be disappointed in the finished product; they just have to trust that the foundation for their dream home is already there, hidden behind the rotted siding and the mildewy purple shag.

Fortunately, that question will never have to be asked of God; he has taken on billions of fixer uppers throughout all of history, beginning with the first two—Adam and Eve—and continuing right on up to you and me. Much worse than bee hives in the walls and fuchsia-colored countertops, God's fixer uppers consist of "corrupt sexual relationships, impurity, unbridled lust, idolatry, witchcraft, hatred, arguing, jealousy, anger, selfishness, contentiousness, division, envy *of others' good fortune,* drunkenness, drunken revelry, and other shameful vices *that plague humankind*" (Gal. 5:19–21). But when his clients trust him and allow the Holy Spirit to renovate their souls, it "produces a different kind of fruit: *unconditional* love, joy, peace, patience, kindheartedness, goodness, faithfulness, gentleness, and self-control" (vv. 22–23).

Too often we are like the Gaines' clients, not able to envision the completed renovation. All we can see are the gaudy chandeliers, the moldy tub, and the dead shrubbery all throughout the yard. But that is not how God views the children whom Psalm 139:13 says he knit together in the womb. Paul wrote in 2 Corinthians 5:17 that "anyone who belongs to Christ has become a new person. The old life is gone; a new life has begun!" (NLT). And he could speak confidently on this because he knew the foundation was already there for each of us, since God "created mankind in his own image" (Gen. 1:27 NIV).

After another successful reno project, this time for the Ivy family, Chip said, "The Ivys took a chance on this place and it's amazing. To purchase this house that had very little potential at all and now you look at it and go, 'Why didn't everybody see this?'"[1]

That's exactly what God says about his children: "Why doesn't everybody see this?" Without him, we have even less potential than the houses being renovated on *Fixer Upper* or any of the other similar shows—in fact, we have none. But with "the God who can do so many *awe-inspiring things, immeasurable things,* things greater than we ever could ask or imagine through the power at work in us" (Eph. 3:20), our market value has skyrocketed.

Without God, we have even less potential than the houses being renovated on *Fixer Upper* or any of the other similar shows—in fact, we have none.

UNDERCOVER **GOD**

> "He didn't look like anything or anyone of consequence—he had no physical beauty to attract our attention. . . . As if he was a person to avoid, we looked the other way; he was despised, *forsaken*, and we took no notice of him."
>
> —Isaiah 53:2–3

As odd as it may sound, the same network that brought us *2 Broke Girls*, *Mike and Molly*, and *$#*! My Dad Says* also gave us a reality show premise that parallels the story of Jesus perhaps more than anything else on television when they premiered *Undercover Boss* after the Super Bowl in February 2010.

The premise is simple: A CEO or other higher-up in a Fortune 500 company temporarily leaves his position, family, and home to immerse himself in lower levels of his company. While undercover, he serves in multiple positions, is bossed around by those who unknowingly work for him, and gets to know a few individuals personally. In the end, he reveals himself and oftentimes gives extraordinary gifts to those he meets, gifts that, in essence, they would never be able to earn for themselves.

Hmm. Where have I seen this before? . . . No, that's not it. . . .

How about in the gospels of Matthew, Mark, Luke, and John?

Two thousand years ago, Jesus, too, temporarily left his position (king), family (God and the Holy Spirit), and home (heaven) and immersed himself in the day-to-day lives of his people. While most did not recognize him as the Messiah, not even his closest friends at first, he was still able to personally touch a handful of people he crossed paths with, giving them gifts they could never earn for themselves—healings, resurrections, exorcisms, and most of all, forgiveness for their sins.

When the CEO of Cinnabon scrubbed dishes and mopped the floors, she was imitating the ultimate servant, Jesus, who washed the feet of his disciples (John 13:2–9).

When a coworker of the undercover boss of Orkin said that the "new trainee" didn't fit the profile of an Orkin man, Jesus may have chuckled, remembering all the scribes and Pharisees who didn't believe he matched what they sought from a messiah (Mark 2:16).

When the undercover boss from Boston Market was disgusted with what she found going on at one of her stores, Jesus probably sympathized with her, remembering when he discovered what was going on at his Father's temple (John 2:13–16).

And when an employee at ADT compared the boss's gracious gift of twenty-five thousand dollars to winning the lottery without even playing,[2] she spoke for all of us who have won the lottery of God's grace and forgiveness with no work whatsoever of our own (Eph. 2:9).

> "He set aside His infinite riches and was born into the lowest circumstances so that you may gain great riches through His humble poverty."
> —2 Corinthians 8:9

Guess Which Family:
THE ROBERTSONS vs. THE KARDASHIANS

CHRISTMAS 2013

1. In which Christmas special (*Duck Dynasty* or *Keeping Up with the Kardashians*) did the women want to do a family Christmas card without the men and children in the family?

2. In which of the two Christmas specials did two men enlarge and frame family pictures for their wives (that included the entire family—what a concept!)?

3. In which Christmas special did the crazy uncle drink sweet tea out of a goblet during a production of the church nativity play?

EARLY ISRAEL-ERA **PAWN**

Today's trash is tomorrow's treasure. At least that's what it feels like when you walk into antique and collectible stores and find the record player you threw out when you got your first '80s-style boom box (that can record from one tape to another as it's being carried on your shoulder!) selling for a hundred bucks. People seem to really love old things, and they'll pay top dollar for them too.

Two recent reality shows, *Pawn Stars* and *Hardcore Pawn*, were quick to realize they could turn the day-to-day interactions of haggling over items ranging from Chinese swords to pinball machines to rejected military vehicles into broadcast hits when people tune in to get history lessons on Charles Lindbergh from the store owner and amusing family bickering over what their Cinco de Mayo party should be like.

4. In which Christmas special did family members drink champagne as they simulated opening gifts on Christmas morning?

5. In which Christmas special was the only mention of "Jesus" the What Would Jesus Do? bracelet one family member gave to another as a white elephant gift?

6. In which Christmas special did one man hunt and kill a hog in order to feed their friends at the church?

7. In which Christmas special did the family spend untold thousands to take a post-apocalyptic photograph to send out to their friends as the family Christmas card?

Answer Key: If you need an answer key, then you haven't watched either of these shows.

But there is certainly nothing new about this love for old. One item that Rick and his dad, "Old Man," would love to get their hands on but could never afford was celebrated long ago when it was discovered among the rubble and shared with the people of Judah: the Book of the Law.

About six and a half centuries before Jesus was born, there was a king named Josiah who took the crown when he was only eight years old. Eighteen years into his kingship, Josiah sent his high priest Hilkiah to lead the restoration of God's temple that had become a home for all sorts of pagan gods during one of his predecessors' reigns. What Hilkiah found upon his initial search through the temple would make sweeping reform in all of Jerusalem: "I have found the Book of the Law in the LORD's Temple!" (2 Kings 22:8 NLT). It is not conclusive what exactly the "Book of the Law" that Hilkiah found was, but most believe it was either an early version of Deuteronomy or perhaps even the entire first five books of the Bible, known as the Pentateuch. Either way, Hilkiah had found the communicated Word of God that had been passed down to Moses hundreds of years earlier and given to the early kings of Israel before getting lost or abandoned, possibly during the evil reign of King Manasseh.

> **The Word of God had been lost and then found— a discovery worth a great deal more than what the fake Claude Monet painting shown to Rick would have been had it been authentic.**

When Josiah was given Hilkiah's great find, he didn't hop on a plane to Las Vegas and visit World Famous Gold and Silver Pawn Shop to see how much he could get for it. Instead, "he tore his clothes in despair" and demanded, "Inquire about the words written in this scroll that has been found. . . . We have not been doing everything it says we must do" (vv. 11, 13 NLT). The Word of God had been lost and then found. A discovery worth a great deal more than what the fake Claude Monet painting shown to Rick would have been had it been authentic.

REALITY SHOWS
WE WISHED WE *Could've Seen*

Naked and Unashamed: A man and woman are placed in paradise and told to be fruitful and multiply. Their Creator walks with them in the garden during the day and teaches them all they need to know to survive. The man even gets to name all the animals he sees. (Not much creativity goes into naming the fly.) But they need to be leery of that suspicious-looking snake.

Our Brother "the Messiah": James and Jude have always been jealous of their big brother Jesus. Their mom and dad treat him as though he can do nothing wrong. With the help of a camera crew, they are on a mission to catch him disrespecting someone or slacking on the job or cheating on his homework . . . anything to help them feel better about their own shortcomings. They may be waiting awhile.

700 Wives and Counting: Poor Solomon. Every day he has a birthday or two to shop for, a few hundred phone calls to make if he's going to be home late from work, and don't even get him started about Mother's Day. He ran out of rose bushes in the royal garden sometime after he married wife number four hundred (ol' what's-her-name). But thank goodness he has three hundred "special friends" to run to when the wives start nagging. Some days seem to never end for Solomon, and neither do the honey-do lists.

What's That Smell? John the Baptist Edition: The son of a priest moves to the desert and wears clothes made from camel hair and lives off of honey and wild locusts. But when he's not swatting his next meal, he's gathering up a merry band of disciples and preparing them for the coming King. Oh, John, you and your crazy backwoods antics. I hope your malnutrition doesn't cause you to go crazy one day and lose your head.

EXTREME MAKEOVER: CHURCH EDITION

"During those days, the entire community of believers was deeply united in heart and soul to such an extent that they stopped claiming private ownership of their possessions. Instead, they held everything in common."
—Acts 4:32

Each week on *Extreme Makeover: Home Edition*, a family was chosen who both serves the community in sacrificial ways and desperately needs help themselves because of a financial, health, or other burden currently placed on them. Over a span of one week, builders, subcontractors who are normally competitors, and hundreds of community volunteers donated their materials, labor, and vacation days to help build a new home for the family in need. Oftentimes they also raised money and other support for a specific ministry of the family that will help them to continue serving the needs of the community they have come to love.

In the end it usually became rather emotional seeing all this come together. And not just for the family being served or for the TV audience trying to avoid letting others see their tears while watching all of this. But it also stirs the heart of God our Creator and Jesus his Son who see these communities giving selflessly and sacrificially all that they can to help others, just as Jesus had intended his church to do so when he left this world.

"This is an awesome responsibility," said the builder in charge of the new home for the Slaughter family in 2009.[3] Yes, indeed, it is an awesome responsibility of the church to give all they can for their brothers and sisters in need.

It was said concerning the week in 2008 when the community helped out the Gaudet family, "This week has been about people working together for the greater cause"[4]—the greater cause, of course, for the church being the glory of God and the sharing of the gospel. And sacrificially serving others is how the church is to do that.

There is a reason why this show touches our hearts as it does: this is how Jesus intended his church to live.

> "Let us consider how to inspire each other to greater love and to righteous deeds, not forgetting to gather as a community, as some have forgotten, but encouraging each other, especially as the day *of His return* approaches."
> —Hebrews 10:24–25

WHO DO YOU THINK YOU ARE: THE **BEAUTIFUL MESS** OF JESUS' GENEALOGY

The NBC and TLC show *Who Do You Think You Are?* may appear to be only a sixty-minute-long Ancestry.com commercial that showcases celebrities researching their family roots, but the sometimes messy family tree each person discovers on their journey is reminiscent to the genealogy God specifically ordained for his Son, Jesus.

Sex and the City actress Cynthia Nixon discovered a great-great-great-grandma who put an ax right through her husband's eyes as he was sleeping one night; *About a Boy*'s Minnie Driver learned of a tangled web while researching the ancestors of the dad she shared with another family; and *The Notebook* star Rachel McAdams learned of a family member who served as a British loyalist during the American Revolution.

As these actresses and others on the show have learned, all the various branches of our family trees say a lot about who we are and what it took to get us to where we are at this point in our lives. McAdams said of her motivation for wanting to find out more about her family, "We also want to create more of a connection for our mom to be able to know these things about her family. . . . It would really help her to be able to put more of the pieces of the puzzle together."[5]

The genealogy of Jesus that Matthew gave us at the beginning of his gospel indeed helps to put the puzzle pieces together for who Jesus is and why he came, simply by merely looking at the women Matthew lists. The inclusion of women in a genealogy list was atypical, since descent was usually traced through men, as they were the head of the family; but Matthew makes a point to add in a few women from Jesus' family tree—ladies who you could say had "questionable" character.

Tamar was Judah's daughter-in-law who, when her mother-in-law died, disguised herself as a prostitute and slept with Judah, becoming pregnant with twins. She made Matthew's genealogy.

Rahab was a prostitute living in the promised land before Joshua and the Israelites invaded the land. She's in the who's who list also.

Bathsheba slept with King David when her husband Uriah was out to war—yep, she made the list.

Ruth was a Gentile from the land of Moab, a land that God called "the washpot in which I rinse *My feet*" (Ps. 60:8). Yet one of the washpot's maidens became the great-grandmother of King David and was part of the Messiah's lineage.

And then of course teenage Mary gave birth to Jesus, the Savior of all these women and the glue that holds all the puzzle pieces together.

When Jason Sudeikis, Rashida Jones, and Kelly Clarkson set out on their quests to find out more about where they came from, there was no guarantee that every branch of their trees would be filled with war heroes and school-teachers. And certainly that is not what they found. But anyone studying Jesus' roots would find more sinners and less saints, and that's exactly how God designed it. Jesus came to redeem all. Prostitutes, ax murderers, and polygamists too.

 CRAZY FAMILIES ARE NOTHING NEW

One day Uncle Si from *Duck Dynasty* is handcuffing himself to his nephew Willie and another day is in a doughnut-induced coma in his new trailer when Jase and the others tow him away into the woods and leave him alone in the middle of nowhere. In *Leah Remini: It's All Relative*, family members bicker and nag each other about whether someone is using words like "rhetorical" and

> **The Kardashians don't own the copyrights to bizarre family quibbles. That honor goes to the first family ever on earth.**

"ambiance" correctly. Kardashian daughters take a cell phone video of their mom going to the bathroom in a public restroom and then post it on their blog. The Wahlbergs, Real Housewives, and Honey Boo Boo—all involving families that draw millions of viewers each week who find themselves strangely curious to see the latest antics of these seemingly disparaging, self-obsessed celebrities of voyeurism. What is Jase going to do today to get on Willie's nerves? How is the Atlanta bride-to-be ever going to be able to find a wedding dress when her mom is throwing her shoe at the bride's best friend in the waiting room? Will Corey and Austin from *Pawn Stars* ever find any of Rick's history lessons not mind-numbingly boring?

But the truth is, the Kardashians don't own the copyrights to bizarre family quibbles. That honor goes to the first family ever on earth. Khloe may have TP-ed and shaving-creamed sister Kim's house, but at least she didn't kill her in a jealous rage like Cain did to his brother Abel (Gen. 4).

And the list of family squabbles throughout the Bible doesn't end there. Immediately after the flood subsided, Noah's son Ham humiliated and dishonored his father when he gossiped to his brothers about the drunkenness of their dad (Gen. 9:20–23). Jacob disguised himself as his brother Esau (under their mother's direction) in order to steal his older brother's blessing from their blind, dying father (Gen. 27). Joseph's older brothers conspired to kill him and leave him in a pit before finally taking pity on him and (like the good big brothers they were) selling him into slavery (Gen. 37:12–28).

And that's just Genesis! In 2 Samuel 13 we read the story too intense for even *20/20* about King David's son Amnon raping his sister Tamar, and then their brother Absalom murdering Amnon in revenge. One might think God should've left out this more extreme example of unbrotherly love from his Book, but he said, "No, let's keep it in there. I want the whole world to read about it." Because there's no disguising the undeniable fact that it's not all bear hugs and fist bumps with family. Even Jesus' family once said of the Messiah, "Jesus has lost His mind" (Mark 3:21).

Guess Who Said It First:
THE THINGS WE SAY THAT YOU NEVER KNEW WERE
from the Bible

▶ Phil Robertson may consider beavers building dams on his land to be the "thorn in his flesh," but they probably aren't as bad as the original unknown thorn the apostle Paul dealt with.

"And lest I should be exalted above measure through the abundance of the revelations, there was given to me a thorn in the flesh, the messenger of Satan to buffet me, lest I should be exalted above measure." (2 Cor. 12:7 KJV)

▶ Miss Kay, as the "apple of Phil's eye," has at least one thing in common with the Old Testament figure Jacob, who was once described in the same way.

"He [God] led him about, he instructed him, he kept him as the apple of his eye." (Deut. 32:10 KJV)

The Kardashians might feel superior to their sisters at times; the Wahlbergs may have thrown a few punches over the years; and everyone knows how much Willie and Jase love to nag their momma's-boy little brother, Jep. But we tune in every week (sometimes like a car wreck that we just can't look away from but know we should) and watch these families deal with each other. Maybe we don't always (or ever) agree with how they're treating their siblings or parents, but we're still drawn to a family dynamic that God established and blesses as they remain loyal to each other in the end.

Many viewers may not have close-knit families at home and they find themselves obsessed with these on-screen family bickerings, wishing that they had a family who cared enough to squabble over such ridiculous things. We can't dismiss that God created the family unit and intended everyone to live within the support of one. Multiple times his Word commands us to take special care of the widows and orphans because he knows the holes that have been torn in their lives with the passing of loved ones. And when Cain murdered his brother, God didn't put an end to the family; instead he gave Adam and Eve another child, Seth. The family was God's intention, no matter what ugliness may arise from it at times.

> The family was God's intention, no matter what ugliness may arise from it at times.

Most of the families we watch on reality television could probably benefit from heeding Paul's words to Timothy: "Respect an elderly man. Don't speak to him sharply; appeal to him as you would a father. Treat younger men as brothers, elderly women as mothers, and younger women as sisters in all purity" (1 Tim. 5:1–2). Sometimes Uncle Si, "Old Man," and Khloe seem to be just asking for their family's disrespect. But one thing all these families have in common is the financial support of those who mean the most to them. Oftentimes the family on television revolves around one who found more financial success than the other members of the family, and he or she is providing for them out of the fruits of their labor. If we're going to throw the above verses from Paul their way in judgment, maybe we should also remember what he said just a few verses later: "Listen, if someone is not providing for his own relatives and especially his own household, then he is denying the faith and is worse off than an unbeliever" (v. 8). Are all God's children watching these families they call train wrecks providing for their families in every way they can too, or are they "worse off than an unbeliever"?

Every family has its crazy uncles and embarrassing skirmishes, not just those with the cameras in front of them. But since the cameras are rolling anyway, we may as well tune in every now and then and see what these established-by-God families are doing today. If there's something to learn from Amnon and Absalom, surely there's redemption to be found in a few of the Real Housewives.

Okay, maybe just one or two of them.

THE DIRTY LITTLE SECRETS Bible QUIZ

1. When Abram (Abraham) and Sarai (Sarah), his wife, went down to Egypt to escape a famine, what did they tell the Egyptians?

    a. That Abram was a leper

    b. That they were actually brother and sister

    c. That God had sent them to punish Egypt

    d. That Sarai was pregnant

2. What did Caleb offer as a reward to the man who attacked and captured Kiriath-sepher?

    a. The right to succeed him as the leader in the land

    b. Whatever part of the land he chose for his inheritance

    c. His daughter

    d. One-half the plunder of the city, after removing the items that must be presented to the Lord's treasure

    e. His "Spider-Man" issue #1 comic book, in primo condition

3. How did Abimelech die?

    a. He accidentally fell on his own sword while running toward the tower at Thebez.

    b. One of his own men hit him over the head with a rock.

    c. He ordered one of his own men to kill him with a sword after being injured by a woman.

    d. Two women of Thebez managed to strangle him with rope.

    e. An iron chariot wheel ran over his head.

4. What curse had Saul uttered during the day of battle?

    a. A curse on any of his men who ate before Saul had gotten vengeance on his enemies

    b. A curse on any man who turned from battle out of fear

    c. A curse on the enemies of the Lord, who were "the uncircumcised worshipers of Dagon"

    d. A curse on Samuel for appointing him as king

5. When Ahaziah became king of Judah, he ruled wickedly. Whose counsel encouraged him to do so?

    a. His wife's

    b. His chief military advisor's

    c. His magic eight ball's (As I see it, "yes.")

    d. A prophet of Baal's

    e. His mother's

Answers: 1) b 2) c 3) c 4) a 5) e

CHAPTER 7

Sing a NEW Song

Before Katy Perry and One Direction wowed the tweens with their Broadway show–like performances. Before Madonna and Prince replaced their last names with songs and dances that made audiences blush. Even before the Beatles and Elvis Presley made women scream by shaking their hair and legs . . . we had the Israelites. That's right—robe-sashaying, sandal-tapping, tambourine-shaking Israelites. Who would've thought the Israelites could teach us still today a thing or two about music?

Since coming to Egypt during the famine of the last chapters of Genesis, the Israelites had been forced into slavery. For four hundred years the Egyptians "violently forced them to work *until they were sore and tired—far beyond exhaustion*. The Egyptians made life bitter for all those Israelites forced to mix mortar, make bricks, and do all types of *grueling* work in the fields. They tormented their Israelite slaves until all the work was done" (Ex. 1:13–14).

As with what happened concerning the Israelites upon escaping Pharaoh, each of us has a God-given desire to celebrate with song and dance.

Then along came Moses, the Israelite shepherd raised as an Egyptian, on a mission from God by way of the burning bush to free the enslaved Israelites from Pharaoh and lead them to the promised land. Pharaoh would not be easy to convince, however, which led to water turning into blood, frogs falling from the sky, gnats and flies on every man and beast, cattle dying, boils on the skin, hail, locusts, and darkness throughout the day. Finally, after the firstborn of every household throughout Egypt, including Pharaoh's home, died at the hand of the Lord, the Israelites were released from slavery.

Pharaoh's change of heart did not last long, though, and he sent six hundred chariots chasing after Moses and the Israelites to bring them back or perhaps destroy them in the desert. With Pharaoh's army at their backs and the Red Sea before them, Moses and the Israelites appeared trapped. But at God's command, Moses stretched out his hand over the sea and a strong wind forced back the waters, allowing them all to cross over onto dry land.

When every Israelite had crossed over safely and Pharaoh's army was well on their way continuing down the newfound Red Sea trail, God brought the waters back down, covering over all the Egyptians and their chariots. Every single one of the pursuing Egyptians perished that day, while all the Israelites stood safely on dry ground.

Four hundred years of slavery. Ten horrifying plagues. A miraculous escape.

And the Israelites' first reaction upon looking back at the Red Sea, with the dead Egyptians underneath and the slavery they had finally been freed from on the other side?

They sang.

They sang about the awesomeness of God, and about the Egyptians swimming at the bottom of the sea who "sank like lead down into the mighty waters" (Ex. 15:10). Then the women all picked up their tambourines and began dancing joyfully. (Suddenly the silliness of Broadway breaking out into song and dance at a moment's notice doesn't seem so crazy, does it?)

After all they had gone through, after all they had seen, their first reaction was not to fall down in exhaustion. It was not to cry from relief. They didn't start jotting everything down into their journals and working on obtaining the movie rights. They didn't give high-fives all around, slapping one another on their butts. They didn't even all join hands in prayer or find the closest church to celebrate in.

They sang a song together and danced.

God intended us to have music in our lives.

* * *

As with what happened concerning the Israelites upon escaping Pharaoh, each of us has a God-given desire to celebrate with song and dance. That may not always look or sound pretty to the rest of the world, but it sure does to God's eyes and ears. On a similar note, today's musicians, whether they realize it or not, have all been gifted by their Creator with the extraordinary talents they are now using to bring music to the world. Combine a God-given desire for song and dance with a God-given talent being used to bring joy to millions, and perhaps we don't have to only look to Christian radio and the Dove Awards to find our Creator in today's music.

At the risk of losing my church membership, I'd like to point out five biblical purposes for music that I still see in much of today's Top 40. I'm not saying the songwriters had the intent to do so or that Ryan Seacrest notices and explains the comparisons every Sunday morning on his weekly countdown. But perhaps today's music isn't as far off from God's intended use of it as we thought.

> Today's musicians, whether they realize it or not, have all been gifted by their Creator with the extraordinary talents they are now using to bring music to the world.

⬇ JOY

Sometimes the pure, unapologetic joy in a person's life can only be expressed in one way—song and dance. The Israelites, for example, sang eighteen impromptu verses after crossing the Red Sea, half of which had to do with the gruesome drowning of their enemies, who "sank to the *muddy* depths like a stone" (Ex. 15:5). And make no mistake, they were quite joyful about it.

Mary, the mother of Jesus, sang her own song of joy shortly after learning of the coming Messiah living in her womb (Luke 1:46–55). "My soul lifts up the Lord! My spirit celebrates God, my Liberator!" she starts off in her song of praise to God, in front of her cousin Elizabeth. As with the Israelites who had just witnessed the Red Sea parting a pathway to freedom, Mary too had just experienced the supernatural, the hand of God in her life in a way that had never been experienced before by anyone, and all she could do was . . . sing.

Songs of joy didn't die out after the New Testament, and they certainly don't reside only on Christian airwaves. One of the biggest songs of 2014 was Pharrell Williams's appropriately titled "Happy." For those who haven't heard the song, basically, Pharrell Williams is pretty happy, which he says twenty-four times in the song by my count. And another twelve times he assures us that nothing can bring him down. (Just Google it and meet me back here in four minutes. I'll wait patiently and sing along in my head. "*Because I'm happy* . . . ")

Catchy song, isn't it? The funny thing about "Happy," though, is that it was first introduced to the world in July 2013 during the end credits of the animated film *Despicable Me 2*. But if you wanted to hear the song a second time, too bad. According to Williams, in an interview with Oprah Winfrey, "the song couldn't get on the radio. . . . Zero air play. Nothing. And the next thing you know, we put out the video on November 21 [2013], all of a sudden, boom!"[1]

**Sometimes the pure, unapologetic joy
in a person's life can only be expressed
in one way—song and dance.**

Heaven, as DEFINED by **SONGS***

"Heaven" by Bryan Adams: Heaven is lying in the arms of his woman.

"Heaven" by Warrant: Heaven is something he's getting closer to every day, as long as his lady friend is with him.

"Heaven" by No Doubt: Heaven is some guy she wants who she also calls her "designer love maker"?

"Heaven" by Uncle Kracker: According to him, heaven better be like Detroit.

*There are roughly one thousand songs with "heaven" in their title, according to www.songlyrics.com. Based on this small sampling, maybe we should simply stick with the Bible to determine what heaven is like.

The song plays in one of the biggest movies of the year . . . nothing. Put out an extremely low-budget video of the song . . . number-one smash hit. Why? Because the video reached the God-given core in every human being, from the Israelites to Mary to everyone today: we just want to sing and dance with joy. The entire video is just Pharrell and countless random people singing along with the lyrics to the song and dancing wherever they are. There is nothing else to it. No special effects. No shaky cam. No mini-film. Just singing and dancing in the streets. And since the premiere of the video, numerous people have posted on YouTube their own versions of the video, also with them simply singing and dancing on the street, at home, at work, wherever. Videos have been sent in from Bermuda, Slovakia, Taiwan, Dakar (yes, *that* Dakar!), Iceland . . . every-where. All of God's children—happy and wanting to share it with the world.

 INSPIRATION

Before each of Ronda Rousey's cage fights in which she'll be fighting off her opponent's choke holds and attempting to hyperextend someone's knee, the MMA fighter walks out to Joan Jett's "Bad Reputation," looking for some last-minute inspiration to help her avoid ankle locks and arm triangles.

When L.A. Angels MVP outfielder Mike Trout walks up to home base looking to hit a baseball no wider than the width of his bat coming toward him at ninety miles per hour, he hopes that songs by Drake and Linkin Park can help put him in the right mind-set.

And runners all over the world make special playlists to listen to as they pound the pavement. They hope their music gives them the inspiration they need to trek up the seemingly insurmountable hill and persevere through their most recent cramp. The right song can do miracles for the exhausted and unmotivated runner.

However, fighters, baseball players, and runners weren't the first ones on God's earth to look to music for inspiration. King David of the Old Testament, who wrote dozens upon dozens of psalms, took down a giant with a single stone, brought the ark of the covenant to Jerusalem, and was Israel's greatest king, was also a musician who understood the power of the song.

"Listen to this, all you people!" he wrote. "Pay attention, everyone in the world! High and low, rich and poor—listen! For my words are wise and my thoughts are filled with insight. I listen carefully to many proverbs and *solve riddles with inspiration from a harp*" (Ps. 49:1–4 NLT, emphasis added).

Many years later, the prophet Elisha also understood what King David did. When the kings of Judah, Israel, and Edom sought out God's guidance over their battle with the king of Moab, they went to Elisha to hear from God. After they pleaded with Elisha for his help, he said to them, "Bring me a musician!" And then the Bible tells us, "While the musician was playing, Elisha was empowered by the Eternal" (2 Kings 3:15). Other Bible versions use the phrase "the hand of the LORD came" upon him (NASB, NIV, NKJV) to describe what happened while the musician played.

Music inspires us today because that is one of the reasons God intended it to be used in the first place. When the latest Black Eyed Peas or Maroon 5 song keeps us on that treadmill for one more mile, we are allowing something created by God to fulfill its purpose of inspiration in us.

Guess Who Said It First:
THE THINGS WE SAY THAT YOU NEVER KNEW WERE
from the Bible

▶ Queen's famous song "Another One Bites the Dust" may have debuted in 1980, but the phrase it stemmed from, "lick the dust," has been around just a tad longer.

"They that dwell in the wilderness shall bow before him; and his enemies shall lick the dust." (Ps. 72:9 KJV)

▶ Bruno Mars, judging from your song "Locked Out of Heaven," I'm not sure you quite understood what Jesus meant by "born again" when he spoke with Nicodemus.

"Verily, verily, I say unto thee, Except a man be born again, he cannot see the kingdom of God." (John 3:3 KJV)

 LOVE

Perhaps the type of song written most often, and certainly the one most enjoyed by its audience, is the love song. If you Google "greatest love songs," you will find countless lists that music fans, magazines, and others have put together. However, almost nobody agrees on what songs should make up that list. A sampling of the top five songs from five different lists showed only three songs that were on multiple lists: "Your Song" by Elton John; "Something" by the Beatles; and "My Girl" from the Temptations. However, those songs are all older than cassette tapes; what about in the iTunes era? Aren't artists such as Maroon 5, Florida Georgia Line, and Bruno Mars finding great success from their love songs?

John Legend has touched a lot of hearts with his song "All of Me." Who wouldn't like being told that they are someone's muse and that even their imperfections are loved? At one lyrics website, posts were made from listeners who said things like, "This song describes true love," and "This love song says no matter who you are, you deserve to be loved for all that you are. . . . John Legend has hit the nail on the head!"[2]

Bruno Mars found a number one hit on the *Billboard* Hot 100, as well as a Grammy award for Best Male Pop Vocal Performance, in his ballad "Just the Way You Are," which also plays on the themes of loving every part of some-one. Mars knows that there's nothing a woman wants more than for a man to look into her eyes and tell her that she is amazing just as she is.

The females of the Top 40 aren't to be ignored either when talking about great love songs of today. Even young Miley Cyrus, in her song "Adore You," understands the language of men when she talks about needing him and ador-ing him. *American Idol* winner and country music star Carrie Underwood puts a smile on her hockey-playing husband, Mike Fisher, when she sings to him in her song "Look at Me" that he is what she has been waiting to find and that she'd do anything he wants her to.

But Bruno, Miley, and the others aren't the only ones who can write a good love song. In fact, the aforementioned "greatest love songs" ever can't even compare to a love song found in the Bible, of all places. Even today's pop singers would swoon and blush if someone had written them a song like what King Solomon and the Shulamite maiden sang for each other. In the appropri-ately titled Song of Songs, we find many such quotes as:

- "Take me away with you; let's run away together!" (1:4).

- "Now, my dove, *don't be shy. Don't hide from me* in the clefts of the rock *or nest like a bird* in secret among the cliffs. Show me your *lovely* form" (2:14).

- "My love is mine, and I am his. He grazes among *my* lilies" (2:16).

- "Your breasts are like two fawns, twin gazelles grazing in a meadow of lilies" (4:5).

🗨 "You are so beautiful, my love, without blemish" (4:7).

🗨 "Your lips *taste sweet* like honey off the comb, my bride; milk and honey are beneath your tongue" (4:11).

🗨 "My insides began to throb for him. I leaped from my bed to let my love in" (5:4–5).

🗨 "Under the apple tree I roused your *love for me*" (8:5).

I don't know about you, but I suddenly have a great love for lilies and apple trees . . . and gazelles.

Ironically, there are many more songs that could've been referenced in this chapter if not for the explicit themes, lyrics, and metaphors; however, King Solomon and the Shulamite set the original bar for arousing emotions between two young lovers, *and then God decided their song was needed in the Bible*. How awesome is that! Suddenly Boyz II Men's "I'll Make Love to You" just isn't racy enough, is it?

↓ RELAXATION

If Only I COULD **TELL . . .**

Bruno Mars that being "locked out of heaven" is a whole lot worse than he thinks (see Bruno Mars's "Locked Out of Heaven").

John Legend that Jesus, too, wants you to give your all to him, including all your imperfections (see John Legend's "All of Me").

Shakira that it doesn't do any good to give our sins to her, only to God (see Shakira's "Empire").

Katy Perry that she hit the nail on the head explaining how much God loves her when she wrote "Unconditionally" (see Katy Perry's "Unconditionally").

Just as there has long been music meant to inspire and motivate you, as well as music that can usually successfully get someone "in the mood," there has also been music throughout time that has been used to help slow life down, put things in perspective, and help one achieve rest, both physically and mentally.

After a long night of studying, college students put on their headphones and try to detach from the pressure by closing their eyes and dozing off to Mumford & Sons. And much cheaper than a spa treatment for ladies who need to check out for a while is the always-inviting chance to soak in a tub while sipping on Zinfandel and listening to stress-relieving playlists filled with the Killdares, Lord Huron, and Colbie Caillat.

Even before spas piped in soft music mixed with sounds of rain to help relax their clients, before malls played relaxing melodies over their speakers to help slow their shoppers down and cause them to shop longer, before elevators used the easy listening station on XM Radio to keep people calm while trapped momentarily inside an 8x8 metal box, the first king of Israel also used music to help with the stress of running a kingdom while at the same time being extremely insecure in his job stability.

In 1 Samuel 16, King Saul's servants said to him, "Look, an evil spirit from God is terrorizing you. Let our lord command that his servants find someone skillful on the harp, so that when this evil spirit from God is bothering you, he will play and ease your mind" (vv. 15–16). So his servants brought him the young David—the one who, unknowingly to Saul, had just been anointed by Samuel as the next king—to serve King Saul with his music. "Whenever God allowed the evil spirit to afflict Saul, David would play the harp, Saul would be relieved of his torment, and the evil spirit would depart" (v. 23).

God gave the soon-to-be greatest king of Israel a gift of playing the harp, which David used to help relax his future enemy and pursuer. It's not clear whether there were lavender-scented candles or bubble baths involved with the king's downtime as well, but when today's stressed find rest and relaxation in the soothing sounds of music, they are once again employing a rarely discussed biblical purpose of music used by the first two kings of Israel.

"Answer me when I call to you, my righteous God. Give me relief from my distress," David would say later to God . . . in a song he wrote (Ps. 4:1 NIV).

TODAY'S Artists HAVE a Q&A with *God*

▶ In their song "Hear Me," the band Imagine Dragons asks if anyone can hear them, for they have a lot on their mind.

"As for me, I look to the LORD for help. I wait confidently for God to save me, and my God will certainly hear me" (Mic. 7:7 NLT).

▶ In their song "Rockstar," the band A Great Big World wants to know if anybody is out there.

"The LORD rules over the floodwaters. The LORD reigns as king forever" (Ps. 29:10 NLT).

▶ In their song "Pompeii," the band Bastille would like to know if they should begin in the rubble or in their sins.

"If we confess our sins, he is faithful and just and will forgive us our sins and purify us from all unrighteousness" (1 John 1:9 NIV).

▶ From our old-school hour, Scott Stapp from Creed would like to know, can you take him higher, to a place with golden streets?

"And I saw the holy city, the new Jerusalem, descending out of heaven. ... And the city street was pure gold" (Rev. 21:2, 21).

HONEST **COMMUNICATION**

"The writers of the Bible are too different from me." "They don't know what I'm going through." "They can't relate to my problems and feelings." Have you ever heard anything like this said before? Have you thought it yourself even? With all the *thees* and *thous, dos* and *don'ts*, miracles and so-called children's tales, many have written off the Bible as a source of truth, joy, relief, and answers.

Instead, they look to their newest playlist for songwriters who know what they're going through and can speak to the grief they are living, and perhaps answer some of the questions on their minds.

And there is some good stuff out there that songwriters are communicating, whether to God or to the sky or just to anyone who might hear them. The band A Great Big World, who entitled their debut album *Is There Anybody Out There?*, can be summed up as two guys knowing there is something bigger than themselves going on in the world. With song titles like "I Really Want It," "Say Something," and "There Is an Answer," they are speaking from their hearts, piercing those of their listeners, simply looking for answers in this "great big world."

> **When Christina Perri wrote in her song "Sea of Lovers" that all her prayers get stifled and go unheard, her honest struggles mimic those of the Old Testament prophet Habakkuk.**

In her album *Head or Heart*, Christina Perri wrote in the inside album cover, "Some days we choose to trust our heads to protect, shield, judge, and save us from the risk of getting hurt and some days we choose to trust our hearts that beat, grow, fall, feel and only want to be loved."[4] The thirteen songs she wrote for this album, including the honestly revealing "Human," deal with this struggle between head and heart.

Other pure, honest moments of communication can be found from many other artists, including Nico & Vinz in "Am I Wrong," who are weary of thinking outside the box and have the ambition to be something real; Avicii's "Wake Me Up," which deals with the burdens of being young and immature, yet still having to carry the weight of the world; and Imagine Dragon's "Bleeding Out," which has communicated multiple meanings to its fans, from dealing with depression, to self-sacrifice, to even a picture of Christ on the cross.[5] Even the Biebs himself can sing a song like "Down to Earth" and touch the hearts of far too many children of divorce.

But if one were to open up the Scriptures and compare with many of these artists' lyrics, it may surprise some to find that oftentimes they are simply rewording the psalmists and other honest Scripture writers who weren't afraid to get dirty with God. When Christina Perri wrote in her song "Sea of Lovers" that all her prayers get stifled and go unheard, her honest struggles mimic those of the Old Testament prophet Habakkuk: "How long, O LORD, must I call for help? But you do not listen! 'Violence is everywhere' I cry, but you do not come to save. . . . Should you be silent while the wicked swallow up people more righteous than they?" (Hab. 1:2, 13 NLT).

Or when in her song "Human" she admits her shortcomings, as she is only human, would she find solace in a song written long before her time that says, "What are mere mortals that you should think about them, human beings that you should care for them?" (Ps. 8:4 NLT).

A Great Big World's plea to "say something" before they give up on their loved one touches the core of any who hear their song, just as the psalmist, David, once begged of God in a similar fashion: "Answer me when I call to you. . . . O LORD, hear me as I pray; pay attention to my groaning. . . . How long, O LORD, until you restore me?" (Pss. 4:1; 5:1; 6:3 NLT).

Other moments of true honesty from the psalmist include:

- "I'm exhausted. *I cannot even speak*, my voice fading as sighs. Every day ends *in the same place*—lying in bed, covered in tears, my pillow wet with sorrow. My eyes burn, devoured with grief" (6:6–7).

- "How long will You forget me? Forever? How long will You look the other way? How long must I agonize, grieving Your absence in my heart every day? How long will You let my enemies win?" (13:1–2).

- "O my God, I cry all day and You are silent; my tears in the night bring no relief" (22:2).

- "My problems go from bad to worse" (25:17 NLT).

- "My guilt has covered me; *it's more than I can handle*; this burden is too heavy for me to carry. . . . I am *completely numb*, totally spent, hopelessly crushed. The agitation of my heart makes me groan" (38:4, 8).

I wonder how many unfamiliar with the Bible would be surprised to find such honest, dirty, humble, frustrating pleas of confusion coming from the heroes of the Bible they once thought lived perfect, unrelatable lives. At the same time, I also wonder how many supposedly avid Bible readers dismiss the same type of communication in today's MTV artists as crass and defiant lyrics that their kids should stay away from.

God desires honest questions from his children, and he promises to give honest answers in return, which may at times seem even more unsettling than the question. (Just ask Habakkuk how God responded to his plea mentioned above.) Let us not fault today's musicians for living up to their half of the deal, as the psalmist once did.

★ ★ ★

Had they been alive today, maybe it's not too farfetched to imagine the celebrating Israelites dancing to Pharrell Williams (and I know they would tap their feet and sing in their cars to Miley's "Party in the U.S.A." and Kelly Clarkson's "Since U Been Gone"—that's a given). I could see King Solomon singing some John Legend to his bride, or young David listening to Avicii upon learning he was going to be the next king. Just because the heroes of the Bible lived before today's music doesn't mean they wouldn't have enjoyed any of it. Perhaps their iTunes libraries would be even more loaded up than many of ours.

God intended us to have music in our lives. If not, then what would he have us dancing to?

> Young women will dance for joy;
> Young men will join them, old ones too.
> For I will turn their mourning into joy.
> I will comfort *My people* and replace their sorrow with gladness.
> —Jeremiah 31:13

THE MUSICAL Kings QUIZ

1. Where in the Bible is the reference to "a rose of Sharon, a lily *found in one of the valleys*"?

    a. Nowhere. It is the name of a nineteenth-century novel.

    b. Song of Solomon 2:1

    c. Psalm 24:3

    d. 1 Thessalonians 4:1–2

2. Why did Saul originally send for David?

    a. He had heard that Samuel had anointed David, and planned to kill him.

    b. He wanted David to play the harp for him.

    c. He wanted to see David's skill in slinging stones.

    d. Saul wanted him for a friend to his son Jonathan.

    e. He wanted to train David to be his successor as king.

3. Why was Michal, David's wife, angry at him?

    a. He continued to take wives and concubines, ignoring her and her children.

    b. She believed he had dishonored Saul, her father, by making a treaty with the Philistines.

    c. She felt he had disgraced himself while celebrating the return of the ark of the covenant.

    d. Every time it was his turn to do dishes, he always had to go fight the Philistines.

    e. She believed he was not taking proper precautions regarding his personal safety.

4. Which of these were part of Solomon's description of his bride? (three answers)

> a. "Your legs are as the pillars of the temple."
> b. "You have dove's eyes."
> c. "Your cheeks are as red as the new wine."
> d. "Your hair is like a flock of goats."
> e. "Your neck is like the tower of David."
> f. "Your front teeth have a gap like David Letterman's."

5. How did Solomon's bride describe her husband to the daughters of Jerusalem? (four answers)

> a. "His cheeks are like a bed of spices."
> b. "His voice is like the north wind."
> c. "His head is like the finest gold."
> d. "His nose is as big as a pyramid."
> e. "His eyes shine like sapphires."
> f. "His locks are as black as a raven."
> g. "His body is carved ivory."

Answers: 1) b 2) b 3) c 4) b,d,e 5) a,c,f,g

CHAPTER 8

THERE'S *More* from the Bible THAN YOU MAY REALIZE

In each chapter there has been a little section called "Guess Who Said It First" with examples of popular phrases used still today that many may not know are actually from the Bible. Though the origins of some of these phrases may be surprising to some, it makes sense that the first mass-produced printed book, as well as the best-selling book of all time, would have placed its fingerprints all over so many aspects of culture, including the things we say. Every day people young and old say things like, "I can't believe this took him by surprise. Couldn't he see *the writing on the wall*?" with no idea whatsoever of its biblical basis from Daniel 5, where God's finger literally wrote a message on King Belshazzar's palace wall that only Daniel could interpret.

There are also many other famous Bible stories and terms that the crowd who grew up going to Sunday school and vacation Bible school probably takes for granted, not realizing there is a growing percentage of the population that doesn't always catch or fully understand when they hear them referenced today. I wonder how many people hear comments about Sodom and Gomorrah or the good Samaritan and feign their understanding because they're too embarrassed to admit they don't get it. Even worse, many times the reference being used is far off from its original meaning or intent, leaving the casual fan to believe Stephen King's *The Stand* is an accurate depiction of the end times.

What follows can serve as a cheat sheet for a few of these Bible references and phrases still found in pop culture today. Many have even found themselves in multiple popular movies, TV shows, and songs, oftentimes with incorrect interpretations, and I hope the brief explanation can help better educate those who have learned the story of David and Goliath only from sports analogies.

THE **ANTICHRIST**

Since the 1976 movie *The Omen*, the term "antichrist" has become predominantly associated in Hollywood with a character who is the son of Satan. In the Al Pacino film *The Devil's Advocate*, this false belief is taken a step further when in the climactic scene at the end, it is revealed that the devil's plan all along has been for his son and daughter to mate together, and that their child would become the Antichrist.

Okay . . .

No wonder the world is so uneducated on the Bible.

The term "antichrist" appears in only four verses in the King James translation of the Bible (none being in Hollywood's favorite book of Revelation, by the way), and all refer to the generic labeling of anyone who denies that Jesus is Lord (i.e., 1 John 2:22: "The liar is the one who says, 'Jesus is not really the Anointed One.' This is the antiChrist, the one denying both the Father and the Son").

Hollywood's "Antichrist" is better known in the scriptures as "the lawless one" (2 Thess. 2:8–9 NIV) or the "beast" (Rev. 13:1). Although we hope that the symbolism of Revelation 13:1 in which the beast has ten horns and seven heads is truly just that, there is little we actually know about him. However,

> *Hopefully it won't surprise many to learn that the original and true meaning of Armageddon has absolutely nothing to do with asteroids, zombies, vampires, viruses, plagues, or the earth's core stopping its rotation.*

we do know that unlike in Hollywood, we cannot stop him from being born, because it is a set-in-stone fact that he will be a central figure on Satan's team in the final days of earth. But his eventual cannonball into the "lake of fire" has also been predetermined (Rev. 20), so there is no chance whatsoever of him winning the final battle.

 ARMAGEDDON

Whether it's zombies taking over the world in *The Walking Dead*, an asteroid heading for Earth that only Bruce Willis can stop, or whatever those creatures were chasing Will Smith in *I Am Legend*, one word has been liberally thrown around to describe Earth's supposed end of days: *Armageddon*. But hopefully it won't surprise many to learn that the original and true meaning of Armageddon has absolutely nothing to do with asteroids, zombies, vampires, viruses, plagues, or the earth's core stopping its rotation. (When was the last time you read an obscure reference to the Hilary Swank movie *The Core*?)

The word's only use in all of the Bible comes in Revelation 16:16—"Then they gathered the kings together to the place that in Hebrew is called Armageddon" (NIV). Other translations call it "Har-Magedon"; both mean "mount of Megiddo." Armageddon, or the mount of Megiddo, will be the site in Israel where the leaders of the earth at the end of the seven-year tribulation, including the Antichrist and the False Prophet, make their final battle against God. According to Revelation 19:20–21, it doesn't go well for them: "The beast [Antichrist] was soon captured along with the false prophet. . . . Both of them were thrown alive into the lake of fire that burns with sulfur. And all who remained met death at the blade of the sword that proceeded from the mouth of the One riding on the *white* horse. All the birds feasted fully on their flesh." So it turns out that it will be birds feasting on flesh, not vampires; nevertheless, the real Armageddon is going to be a little unpleasant for the bad side.

 **DAVID** AND GOLIATH

Every time a lesser-known college basketball team goes up against a power-house school like Kentucky or North Carolina during March Madness, at least one sports commentator will throw out the "David versus Goliath" comparison.

Whenever Hollywood depicts a fresh, puppy-faced, likeable lawyer who goes up against a giant, evil corporation á la Erin-Brockovich, "David verses Goliath" will oftentimes be said at least once to describe the massive lopsided-ness of the opposing legal teams.

And when the boxing analyst in *Rocky IV* said, "The Russian towers above the American. It's a true case of David and Goliath,"[1] that actually did not nearly give enough credit to David's incredible feat over the giant, found in the Old Testament book of 1 Samuel. According to IMDb.com, Sylvester Stallone stands just above five foot nine, while the actor playing the Russian boxer, Dolph Lundgren, is listed at six foot five—about eight inches taller than Stallone. However, while young David was probably a good deal taller than Stallone, perhaps even closer to Lundgren's height (as he was offered the armor of King Saul, one of the tallest men in the land), that still pales in comparison with the giant Goliath, "who was over nine feet tall" (1 Sam. 17:4). No, there will never again be a "true case of David and Goliath." The teenager who took down a giant three feet taller than him with a single stone and then cut off his head is a one-and-done deal.

The term "antichrist" appears in only four verses in the King James translation of the Bible (none being in Hollywood's favorite book of Revelation, by the way).

THE **David** QUIZ:
GOOD, BAD, and UGLY

1. How did David happen to be in the army camp when he heard the taunting of Goliath?

    a. He was delivering food to the soldiers.

    b. He was tending sheep when God called him to go to the place of battle.

    c. He was accompanying Saul as part of his training to be king.

    d. He was reporting on the battle for CNN.

    e. He was appointed to sound the trumpet signals for the Israelite army.

2. David told Saul that he (David) was a worthy opponent for Goliath. What were his reasons?

    a. God has promised David he would live to be old; David was one of the better fighters in Saul's army.

    b. His ability to sling stones would allow him to keep Goliath at a safe distance; his spear throwing arm was very strong.

    c. Although he was much smaller, he was also younger and able to move more quickly; Goliath had poor eyesight and would not be able to see David's quick movements.

    d. While protecting sheep, he had killed both lions and bears; the Lord would protect him.

    e. He used to be in roller derby; he was a superstar whom they would never dare injure.

3. Why did David refuse to use the armor offered to him before his battle with Goliath?

    a. It was untested.

    b. It was the wrong color.

    c. It was too large.

    d. It was obsolete.

4. After David committed adultery with Bathsheba, he received word from her that she was pregnant. What was his first plan to solve the "problem"?

    a. To have her husband, Uriah, killed in battle

    b. To bring her husband from battle to sleep with her

    c. To beg Uriah's forgiveness, and offer to make him commander of all his armies

    d. To conspire with Bathsheba and fabricate a story that she was sexually assaulted by a stranger

5. Who came to David and rebuked him for his sin with Bathsheba?

    a. Nathan

    b. Joab, his military commander

    c. His wife Michal (Saul's daughter)

    d. An angel of the Lord

    e. His twelve mothers-in-law

Answers: 1) a 2) d 3) a 4) b 5) a

"DOUBLE-EDGED **SWORD**"

An often-used phrase today that refers to something that can have both favorable and unfavorable consequences, "Double-Edged Sword" was even the title for a season five episode of *30 Rock*, in which über-Republican Jack Donaghy was facing the blessing of a newborn child, albeit in Canada, a country he despises because of its politics.

Long ago King Solomon wrote to his son to be cautious of a "seductive woman." He warned that "in the end, she is bitter . . . she cuts as deep as a double-edged sword" (Prov. 5:4). And Hebrews 4:12 uses the same phrase to describe the Word of God, calling it "alive and moving; sharper than a double-edged sword; piercing the divide between soul and spirit."

Who knew that the same phrase could be used to describe the Bible, a temptress, and a half-Canadian baby?

"EYE FOR AN **EYE**, TOOTH FOR A **TOOTH**"

In a world that loves justice, it doesn't take long for one to first hear and then later use himself the phrase "eye for an eye." Physical harm can lead to retaliation of more physical harm. An act of marital unfaithfulness may lead to one by the offended. And anytime a baseball pitcher throws a ball anywhere near a batter's head, it's almost a given that the opposing pitcher will intentionally do the same in the next inning. "An eye for an eye," the retaliator will often say to justify his actions.

The original use of this phrase, found in Deuteronomy 19:21—"Show no pity: life for life, eye for eye, tooth for tooth, hand for hand, foot for foot" (NIV)—was not written about revenge, however. The law that God handed down to Moses was intended to prevent someone from falsely testifying about another. Basically, if Bob the Israelite was found to have been falsely accusing his neighbor of stealing his sheep, then whatever the punishment would've been for the thieving neighbor had he been guilty is now Bob's punishment—an eye for an eye, tooth for a tooth. (See the later section "Go the Extra Mile" to read about how Jesus referenced this law during his Sermon on the Mount, and what he says is the new law of retaliation.)

"FIGHT THE **GOOD FIGHT**"

In Glee, this phrase was used to encourage the members of the Celibacy Club to stay strong in their commitment to abstinence. In *X2: X-Men United*, Magneto asked Professor X if he was still fighting the good fight in his quest to bring harmony between mutants and humans. And in the movie adaptation of the Nicholas Sparks novel *The Lucky One*, a judge up for reelection claimed to be fighting the good fight for the future of his town.

The uphill battle each of these characters was referring to was nothing compared to the one ahead of Paul's protégé Timothy, to whom Paul wrote, "Fight the good fight of the faith! Cling to the eternal life you were called to when you confessed the good confession before witnesses" (1 Tim. 6:12). This phrase that was used originally as an evangelical call to believe in and spread the Christian faith has become the go-to slogan for anyone encouraging someone to persevere in whatever it is they believe is their "good fight."

But, hey, it worked for Timothy, who played a prominent role in the early spread of Christianity despite the persecution surrounding the first Christians, so why wouldn't it help the Celibacy Club?

"**FORBIDDEN** FRUIT"

This well-known term has been used throughout history to describe anything that was tempting yet dangerous, oftentimes sexual in nature. No doubt *Glee's* Celibacy Club "fought the good fight" in order to flee from the forbidden fruit to which many of their classmates had already succumbed. And many a man or woman has described someone they were highly attracted to but for one reason or another could not ever be with as their own "forbidden fruit."

Interestingly, though, the biblical origin of this term that stems from the garden of Eden has nothing to do with sex. In Genesis 2:16–17, God told

Adam, "Eat freely from any *and all* trees in the garden; I only require that you abstain from eating the fruit of *one tree*—the tree of the knowledge of good and evil." But of course, the forbidden fruit was too much for Adam and Eve to handle, and they caved in the first time a snake told them it was okay to do so.

Culture is also prone to associate apples as the forbidden fruit, when in fact the Genesis passage never shares what type of fruit it was they ate. Two possible reasons for this popular association are that John Milton's epic poem *Paradise Lost* (c. 1677), ten thousand lines of verse to describe Adam and Eve's Eden story, uses an apple as the forbidden fruit, which may have had profound influence on later thought; and also the Latin words for both "apple" and "evil" are identical—*malum*. Since Adam and Eve's disobedience of eating the forbidden fruit is what has become known as the fall of man, it could also be said that this time is when evil entered man's nature; therefore, we have the forgivable association of *malum* (apples—a type of fruit) leading to *malum* (evil).

"GO THE **EXTRA MILE**"

Washington Redskins quarterback Robert Griffin III talked about being willing to go the extra mile in the NFL in order to succeed since everyone in the league already has talent. Actress Anna Kendrick used the phrase to describe her *Up in the Air* costar George Clooney.[2] And motivational speakers everywhere fire up their crowds with clichés like "Go the extra mile. It's never crowded."

The popular encouragement derives from the ultimate motivational speaker, Jesus, who was talking at the time about how we should handle dealing with our enemies. Immediately after reminding the crowd of another still-popular phrase, "an eye for an eye and a tooth for a tooth," he explained that was not the mind-set they should have concerning retaliation: "If someone strikes you on the right cheek, you are to turn and offer him your left cheek. . . . If someone forces you to walk with him for a mile, **walk with him for two instead**" (Matt. 5:39, 41; emphasis added).

Jesus was referencing the common practice at the time of Roman soldiers enlisting anyone they saw while traveling with the job of carrying their equipment for them up to a mile. But Jesus told his audience this day to not only walk with them for the mile the law demands of them, but to "walk with him for two instead."

There is certainly nothing to be taken away from the person who "goes the extra mile" in his efforts to do something, but we should be reminded that the phrase's origin refers not to doing more of something we already love to do, but rather more of what we are being forced to do in order to better love our enemy.

THE **GOOD** SAMARITAN

In the final episode of *Seinfeld*, the gang is stranded in Latham, Massachusetts, when they witness a carjacking and refuse to help out the victim. To their surprise, a police officer later comes to them and says that they're under arrest for breaking Article 223-7 of the Latham County Penal Code, otherwise known as the Good Samaritan Law.

"Good Samaritan" is a label that is oftentimes applied to someone who helps out another. But I wonder how many people familiar with the term (even those in Latham, Massachusetts) know the whole story concerning Jesus' parable from Luke 10, which he shared in order to better answer the question "Who is my neighbor?"

For the emphasis behind Jesus' story is not simply that a Samaritan helped out another person, but that he went above and beyond to assist a Jewish man, someone whom, culturally speaking, it would've been unthinkable for him to help, because "Jews, you see, have no dealings with Samaritans" (John 4:9). And not only did the Samaritan give assistance to someone his friends would've most likely never had any association with, but before he came along two Jewish men, a priest and a Levite, saw the man and ignored him.

Culture is prone to associate apples as the forbidden fruit, when in fact the Genesis passage never shares what type of fruit it was they ate.

Flash-forward two thousand years, and Jerry and Kramer find themselves in prison for doing the same thing. Some people will never learn.

"HE WHO **LIVES** BY THE SWORD, **DIES** BY THE SWORD"

This is a popular peace-promoting phrase that is usually intended to share one's opinion that people who commit violent acts will encounter violence themselves. Though it may sound like something taken straight out of *Hamlet* or *Robin Hood*, the origin is actually from the mouth of the Messiah, Jesus himself, in Matthew 26. When the soldiers seized Jesus after Judas had turned him over to them, Peter immediately unsheathed his sword and cut off the ear of one of the men. But Jesus was quick to dampen Peter's hasty escape plan, telling him, "Put your sword back in its place . . . for all who draw the sword will die by the sword" (v. 52 NIV). And Luke 22:51 tells us that Jesus then touched the man's ear and healed it.

Jesus was not making an antiwar political statement but rather reminding his disciple that God's will was, in fact, being carried out here. He would go on to tell Peter that he had the power to ask his Father to send twelve legions of angels to fight on his behalf; he did not need Peter and his single blade. Jesus had great plans for Peter involving the birth of the church that did not include Peter's dying right then and there.

 **JUDAS** ISCARIOT

Betrayers all throughout pop culture are oftentimes referred to as a "Judas," the name of the disciple who betrayed Jesus, although none have been guilty of betrayal anywhere near to the extent of Judas turning over his friend and Messiah to the authorities, which led to an innocent man's trial and crucifixion. In *The Office* episode "Koi Pond," Dwight labels his coworker Jim a Judas when it is learned that Jim opted to not save their boss, Michael, from falling into the koi pond in an office lobby.

Perhaps one of the more sly Judas references can be found in the season three episode of *The Big Bang Theory* entitled "The Large Hadron Collision." Sheldon feels betrayed when his best friend and roommate, Leonard, decides to bring his girlfriend, Penny, to Switzerland with him when he is offered the chance to visit the CERN laboratory, something Sheldon has always dreamed of doing. Later on in the cafeteria, the betrayed Sheldon brings Leonard thirty pieces of silverware and walks away. This is a clever reference to the thirty pieces of silver Judas Iscariot received in return for betraying Jesus. Thank goodness for laugh tracks. I can't imagine a studio audience would've caught that one.

THE REAL Judas QUIZ

1. What reason did Luke give for Judas's betrayal of Jesus? (two answers)
   a. Judas was angry when he realized Jesus was not going to establish a "physical" kingdom at that time.
   b. He stated that Judas betrayed Jesus "out of greed."
   c. Judas hoped to gain favor with the chief priests.
   d. Luke said that "Satan entered Judas."
   e. He stated that Judas was jealous of Jesus' power.

2. John's account stated that Judas came with a detachment of troops and officers to arrest Jesus. He asked them who they were seeking, and they answered, "Jesus of Nazareth." After He replied, "I am He," what happened?
   a. Judas kissed Jesus on the cheek.
   b. The troops drew back and fell to the ground.
   c. A soldier quickly grabbed Jesus and shackled his hands.
   d. His disciples ran away in various directions.
   e. Jesus was read his Miranda rights.

3. To what reward did Judas agree, for betraying Jesus to the chief priests?

    a. Two talents of gold

    b. A high position in the temple treasury

    c. Thirty pieces of silver

    d. Appointment as personal attendant to Caiaphas, the high priest

    e. A book deal and possibly a movie

4. Whom did the apostles choose to replace Judas?

    a. Jude

    b. Joseph

    c. Matthias

    d. Alf

5. What did Judas do shortly after he betrayed Jesus? (two answers)

    a. Returned the thirty pieces of silver out of remorse

    b. Turned in disciples Peter, James, and John to the authorities as well

    c. Found Jesus and begged him for forgiveness

    d. Hanged himself in a field

    e. Ran away to Nineveh with his newfound wealth

Answers: 1) b,d 2) b 3) c 4) c 5) a,d

"**JUDGMENT** DAY"

As everyone knows, Judgment Day refers to when Skynet launched nuclear missiles at Russia, who responded with a nuclear counterattack against the United States, leading to a nuclear war where three billion people were killed and artificial intelligence took over the world, eventually creating cyborg killers called Terminators who hated all people with the last name of Connor.

While the Judgment Day in the Terminator series actually is not going to happen . . . I think . . . the popular phrase "Judgment Day" is taken straight out of the Bible, which refers on multiple occasions to the "day of judgment." In Matthew 12:36, Jesus said, "I tell you this: on the day of judgment, people will be called to account for every careless word they have ever said." And the apostle Peter wrote, "The heavens and earth *we see* now are being reserved for *destruction by* fire, preserved until the time comes for the godless on the day of judgment" (2 Peter 3:7).

> **While the Judgment Day in the Terminator series actually is not going to happen . . . I think . . . the popular phrase "Judgment Day" is taken straight out of the Bible.**

The Day of Judgment in these verses and others refers to the second coming of Jesus, when he returns to earth to separate his children from those who rejected him. His children he will bring home to heaven, and the others will face the eternity apart from God that they willingly chose. You can find out more concerning the Day of Judgment in Jesus' sheep and goats story found in Matthew 25:31–46.

THE **PRODIGAL** SON

Robin Hood returns to England after fighting in the Crusades with King Richard. In *Iron Man*, Tony Stark takes over as CEO of Stark Industries after going to MIT and presumably living the wild life for a few years. Woody from *Toy Story* is reunited with Jessie and the Prospector. Bill Paxton returns to Oklahoma to get his wife to sign the divorce papers in *Twister*. They are all labeled "prodigal sons." And the only thing they have in common (besides being someone's son—scratch that, Woody didn't have a father) is that they are returning home. Apparently, that is all it takes to be labeled a prodigal son in pop culture.

But the phrase "prodigal son" is taken from a parable of Jesus, found in Luke 15. The true (but, yes, fake, since it is a parable) prodigal son was the son of a wealthy man who asked for his inheritance before his father's death and, upon receiving it, left home and partied like a rock star. But when he ran out of all his money, he took a job feeding pigs, before finally gathering up enough humility to return home to his father, who was waiting for him with open arms.

That doesn't sound like Robin Hood, Tony Stark, Woody, or a divorcing tornado chaser in the least. In fact, none of those men were even returning home to their fathers, which was the key to Jesus' parable: that no matter where his children have gone or what they have done while away, God the father is searching for them, ready to embrace them with open arms.

 ## "REAP WHAT YOU **SOW**"

This common saying is usually hurled out at someone with much spite, basically telling them that the negative consequences they were going to "reap" were because of the terrible things they had "sowed." Even *Survivor* named one of their episodes famous for broken alliances and peeving off fellow castaways "Reap What You Sow."

But the biblical origin of this phrase—"A man reaps what he sows" (Gal. 6:7 NIV)—was actually intended to emphasize more on the positive. In the verses leading up to Paul's now-famous saying, he warned believers who see a brother or sister struggling with a sin, "*Don't stand idle and watch his demise. Gently restore him, being careful not to step into your own snare*" (v. 1). We are to help them, he commands, not say, "Hah! You're finally reaping what you've been sowing!"

Paul then concluded the thought with, "May we never tire of doing what is good and right before our Lord because in His season we shall bring in a great harvest if we can just persist. So seize any opportunity *the Lord gives you* to do

good things *and be a blessing* to everyone, especially those within our faithful
family" (vv. 9–10).

"You reap what you sow" was meant to be an encouragement to ourselves
when persevering through the high roads in life, not an admonishment to
others we see doing things we disapprove of.

 SODOM **AND** GOMORRAH

Comedian and late-night talk show host Jay Leno once quipped, "If God
doesn't destroy Hollywood Boulevard, he owes Sodom and Gomorrah an
apology."[3] This is only one of a seemingly infinite number of references made
throughout history comparing places of wild debauchery (Hollywood and
Las Vegas usually get most people's votes) to the two cities God destroyed
by raining down sulfur and fire from heaven. But let's really hope that neither
Hollywood, Las Vegas, nor any other place in the world today could truly ever
compare with what was going on in these cities from Abraham's day.

Genesis 13:13 says that "the people of *the city of* Sodom were quite
wicked—utterly defiant toward God." Later, God told Abraham concerning the
citizens of Sodom and Gomorrah, "Their sin has become a serious problem"
(Gen. 18:20), and he sent two angels to Lot's house in Sodom to check it out.
While the angels were there, the men of Sodom pester Abraham's nephew,
Lot, outside his house to send the angels out so that they could . . . "get to
know them" . . . intimately . . . yes, the angels from heaven.

And according to a conversation between God and Abraham in Genesis
18, there were not even ten righteous people in the city where "neighbors
were defeated by their own sexual perversions as they pursued the strange and
unnatural impulses of the flesh" (Jude v. 7). Therefore God brought down the

> **"You reap what you
> sow" was meant to be an
> encouragement to ourselves
> when persevering through the
> high roads in life.**

power of heaven on the two cities, "reducing them to ash as a lesson of what He will do with the ungodly in the days to come" (2 Peter 2:6).

But sorry, Jay Leno, the "ungodly in the days to come" is not a reference to those walking the streets of Hollywood Boulevard. See the "Armageddon" and "Judgment Day" sections in this chapter to find out more of what Peter was warning of here.

 ## "THE TRUTH SHALL **SET YOU FREE**"

This is a common saying in pop culture, typically found in academic circles in order to promote educational freedom and the power of learning, as well as in courtrooms, real and fictional, referring to how the actual truth concerning the alleged crime will set the innocent person free. However, neither of these popular interpretations is anywhere close to the original intent of the saying. In John 8:31–32, Jesus told his disciples, "If you hold to my teaching, you are really my disciples. Then you will know the truth, and the truth will set you free" (NIV).

The teaching he was referring to is from the preceding verses: "You are from below; I am from above. You are of this world; I am not of this world. I told you that you would die in your sins; if you do not believe that I am he, you will indeed die in your sins. . . . When you have lifted up the Son of Man, then you will know that I am he and that I do nothing on my own but speak just what the Father has taught me" (vv. 23–24, 28 NIV). So he was telling his followers that when they hold to these things just taught, then they will truly be his disciples. They will know the truth, and the truth will set them free. Later, in John 14:6, he adds, "I am the way and *the truth* and the life. No one comes to the Father except through me" (NIV, emphasis added).

Jesus is the truth. Not education. Not freedom. Not courtroom justice. Only Jesus can set us free. And not free from prison, or from ignorance. But free from the bondage of sin.

"WALK **THROUGH** THE VALLEY OF THE **SHADOW** OF DEATH"

This is another popular phrase to throw around, perhaps most famously as the opening line of Coolio's song "Gangsta's Paradise." It also makes an appearance in a season two episode of *Lost*, entitled appropriately "Psalm 23," when Mr. Eko and Charlie burn the skeleton remains of Mr. Eko's brother inside the plane that crashed on the island many years before. I only wish Mr. Eko and Coolio would've found comfort in the words that follow this popular ominous saying: "Yea, though I walk through the valley of the shadow of death, I will fear no evil; for thou art with me; thy rod and thy staff they comfort me" (Ps. 23:4 KJV). God is with us as we walk through the valley, as King David found when he wrote this psalm, and we can always look to him for comfort, even while still in the valley.

★ ★ ★

If given the space, much more could be written on all the phrases and stories from the Bible that continue to circulate in contemporary culture, well more than the few listed here, including: "cross to bear" (Luke 14:27), "fly in the ointment" (Eccl. 10:1), "wit's end" (Ps. 107:27), "in the twinkling of an eye" (1 Cor. 15:52), "pride goes before a fall" (Prov. 16:18), and "straight and narrow" (Matt. 7:13–14). Some have maintained their original meaning; many have been bent and twisted to meet the needs of the ones saying them. But the fact remains: God's Word that he communicated through roughly forty different authors during a time span of fifteen hundred years has buried itself deep into our culture; so deep, in fact, we oftentimes don't even know that we're quoting it.

> So it is when I declare something.
> My word will go out and not return to Me empty,
> But it will do what I wanted;
> it will accomplish what I determined.
> —Isaiah 55:11

AFTERWORD

All You Want to Know about (Half) the Bible in Pop Culture

I've watched a lot of movies and television in my lifetime, as well as listened to a ton of music. Some reading this may believe I've toed very closely, and perhaps over the edge at times, to the whole "be *in* the world, not *of* the world" admonition Jesus gave his people (see John 17:13–19). And I'm sure I have at times. In fact, I know I have, because as the years pass there continue to be types of movies and shows I once loved that I decide to refrain from watching anymore, as well as radio stations that lose their preset spot in my car.

But that doesn't take away from the greatness of much of the art God's created beings continue to bring their fans every year. There are truly gifted people writing, directing, casting, acting, singing, and dancing all throughout the entertainment industry, who are not to be written off simply because someone may not approve of all the content of their art. At the very least, these artists recognize their amazing talents and are using them to bring joy to many around the world—something many Christians today should try doing more of themselves.

Many concerns and complaints about pop culture found among the church today center around the belief that the artists don't take the ideas far enough. Or perhaps the metaphors and imagery that had held up so strong for the majority of the film unravel at the end, apparently spoiling it all for the audience hoping the gospel to be portrayed perfectly.

The afterlife in *Lost* was more universalistic than gospel-centered, and that did not sit well with many, nor did something similar in the final Harry Potter novel. When Harry wakes up after being apparently killed by Voldemort and finds himself in the not-coincidentally named King's Cross train station, he asks long-deceased Dumbledore where he thinks they really are. "My dear boy," Dumbledore responds, "I have no idea. This is, as they say, *your* party."[1]

Was author J. K. Rowling insinuating, through Dumbledore, her opinion of the afterlife being different for everyone, depending on one's religion? Perhaps some thought so.

When Princess Anna in *Frozen* needed an act of true love to save her from death, her salvation came not from someone offering their own life up for hers but from her sacrificing her own life for her sister, Elsa. It was her own actions that saved her life, not someone else's, which doesn't gel with what Paul wrote in Ephesians 2:8–9: "For it is by grace you have been saved, through faith—and this is not from yourselves, it is the gift of God—not by works, so that no one can boast" (NIV). But does this inaccurate picture of salvation dilute the power of Anna's sacrifice for her sister or the parallels of Elsa as a prodigal child?

And the flaws many have pointed out in movies such as *Bruce Almighty*, *Signs*, and *Book of Eli* were dealt with in detail in chapter 2. There are no perfect movies out there, and there never have been. But does that mean that nothing in these movies can be redeemed for God's kingdom? Hopefully your conclusion is now the same as mine: absolutely not.

If one desires the entirety of the Bible, he should go to . . . well, the Bible. But can't pop culture be used successfully to help people get started in that direction, even if it would be more accurate to label something as "half the Bible" in pop culture? Pop culture is oftentimes quite successful at providing for us the half that recognizes our brokenness. The half that admits our need for love, for purpose. The half that tells us we need redemption, someone or something to save us.

The world's love for superheroes may indeed show the areas in our lives and our world where we cannot do it on our own, where supernatural intervention is absolutely necessary for our survival. But the broken and flawed superhero can only do so much. He may succeed at times, but will often not show up for others or sometimes even fail despite his best efforts. In fact, he too needs a savior. We only have half the Bible here.

A show as great as *Lost* is wonderful at revealing the universal need for redemption in all of us. A plane crashes on a mysterious island, and for six years we see all the survivors' ugly pasts and how they find what they need on the island to overcome what has haunted them and kept them off purpose for too long. But the path to redemption is not very clear. In fact, it's different for each character. We are shown that each of our characters needs some type of saving, and most get it in the end. But how? We only have half the Bible here.

Bruce Almighty shows us we need grace and a supreme being directing our lives, but what then? Is it enough to simply recognize that? How do we receive that grace, and what does following our Maker mean for us? *Signs* made it clear that all things have a purpose, but what is that purpose (beyond killing an alien with water and a baseball bat)? There must be more to why we are here and why certain trials come into our lives. There's only half the Bible to be found in these movies.

Even the 2014 biblical epic *Noah* gave us a Noah who held no hope for the future. He clearly recognized man's sinful downfall and the need for God's intervention, but he could not see past man's failures. In his eyes, man had turned their backs on God and there was nothing that could save them. When Noah and his family stood together on the mountains of Ararat after the flood had subsided and their mission to replenish the earth had begun, how did Noah know that this time would be different? Where would redemption come from when man inevitably messed up again? (And how were they going to "be fruitful and multiply" with the film's decision to not provide wives for Ham and Japheth?) There is certainly a lot of truth to the fictional Noah's perspective, but again, it's only half the Bible.

Fans of *Harry Potter* and *Frozen* know the power of sacrificial love. Indeed the unselfish act of sacrifice by a mother or a sister can save us . . . for a time. But Harry Potter and Elsa will eventually die one day. Their family members can't save them forever. What about the sacrifice that can save for eternity? We only have half the Bible here.

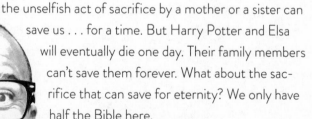

Perhaps nothing is greater at giving us half the Bible than today's music. In the worst of it, we have sinners in full force, partying it up like Sodom and Gomorrah (well, not quite that bad—see "Sodom and Gomorrah," chapter 8). In the best of it, we have bands like A Great Big World posing questions in the form of an album title like *Is There Anybody Out There?* Christina Perri sings that she's only human, and Katy Perry writes about unconditional love. The band Imagine Dragons speaks of the demons inside each of us driving our greed.

Behind this admission of guilt, this search for purpose, this overwhelming need for love found in so much of today's music is . . . I don't know. There are rarely answers given. Again, we only find half the Bible.

Or when an answer is given, whether in a movie or TV show, or on the radio, it's usually the generic answer "love." Just love each other. . . . You only need love. . . . Only love can help us. And then the next song played or the next TV show advertised explains that love means sex. Which people take to heart, try and find "love," and then end up crooning about all of their problems again that just keep repeating themselves.

And repeating themselves.

And repeating themselves.

Because even the best of pop culture today can only give us half the Bible. And that's okay.

They're onto something with their answer of "love," though. Unfortunately, they just haven't been told where to find it. But the answer is the second half of the Bible. The half we won't typically find in Hollywood or on iTunes. The half that gives us the redemption we all need. The half where we are freely given the grace and forgiveness we try so hard to earn on our own. The half that answers the questions we have: Is there anybody out there? Why am I here? Why did this happen to me? The half where the real Noah could find mankind's hope. The half where sacrificial lambs are no longer necessary; the ultimate sacrifice has already taken place. The half that says it's okay that we're only human and that we are deeply flawed, because the Author of Love's "power is made perfect in weakness" (2 Cor. 12:9). The half that can be summed up in one word.

Jesus.

The most important half.

The half that gives meaning to the first half.

* * *

The night before his death, Jesus told those closest to him:

> As the Father has loved me, so have I loved you. Now remain in my love. If
> you obey my commands, you will remain in my love, just as I have obeyed
> my Father's commands and remain in his love. I have told you this so that
> my joy may be in you and that your joy may be complete. My command is
> this: Love each other as I have loved you. Greater love has no one than this:
> to lay down one's life for one's friends. You are my friends if you do what I
> command. I no longer call you servants, because a servant does not know
> his master's business. Instead, I have called you friends, for everything that I
> learned from my Father I have made known to you. You did not choose me,
> but I chose you and appointed you to go and bear fruit—fruit that will last—
> and so that whatever you ask in my name the Father will give you. This is my
> command: Love each other. (John 15:9–17 NIV)

"I have told you this so that my joy may be in you and that your joy may be complete." Even the best of pop culture does not bring lasting joy, nor does it usually claim to. We need joy in our lives, yes. We need to do what's necessary to find joy, sure. But here's where your joy can be completed? We won't find that offered outside of Jesus. Instead, the world says it's up to you. It looks differently for everyone, so good luck with all that, they say. Maybe you'll find your joy completed in a job, or on a vacation, or on an adventure like the day-dreaming title character does in *The Secret Life of Walter Mitty*. Most likely, you'll find it in a man or woman who will stare at you unceasingly and say things like Gus says to Hazel Grace in *The Fault in Our Stars*: "You trying to keep your distance from me in no way lessens my affection for you."[2] *Oh,* we swoon to ourselves, *if only I could have someone love me like that, then my joy would be complete. I'm sure of it.* The first half of the Bible tells us we need joy; the second half completes that joy.

"Greater love has no one than this, that he lay down his life for his friends." Everyone wants to be loved, and pop culture has a different answer for where to find it, depending on what is bringing in the highest-paying advertisers or producing the most popular hashtag. The world clearly acknowledges its great need for love; pretty much everything we watch or listen to today confirms that. But answers are rarely given, and when they are, they're part of a fluffy, generic, build-your-own love sundae. But 1 John 4:8 says clearly that "God is love." And Jesus displayed the ultimate example of love when he laid down his life for his friends—for us. For those reading the first half of the Bible given to us in pop culture and saying they wish they had someone in their lives who loved them enough to sacrifice themselves for them, look to the second half of the Bible—Someone already has.

"My command is this: Love each other as I have loved you." Today's artists and pop culture icons have the greatest intentions when they claim the answer is to simply love others. And indeed they are half right. But the key is to love others . . . as Jesus loves us. Unselfishly. Unconditionally. Eternally. Sacrificially. This doesn't mean that Beyoncé, Katy Perry, Justin Timberlake, or Ariana Grande aren't capable of writing great love songs or that the relationships depicted in *The Fault in Our Stars*, *Twilight*, and *The Notebook* are not genuine. But all humans have one glaring defect: we are human. And loving someone as Jesus loves us is not part of a human's default in-store setting. Again, the first half of the Bible is great at recognizing our need for that kind of love, but the second half is where we find it, and where we learn how we have been commanded and can be made capable to love others in that way too.

★ ★ ★

All You Want to Know about Half the Bible in Pop Culture. It just doesn't ring the same, does it? Plus, no one wants half of something. When Jerry Seinfeld began keeping a list of all the grocery items that his mooching neighbor Kramer helped himself to, he had to break the news to him: he didn't want half of the apple Kramer had left for him, the remaining half of the opened can of Coke, or half of a banana. It's either all or nothing!

We also don't typically watch half a movie, even if it's pretty bad. Or read half a book, download half a song, and do half the job our bosses or parents ask of us. We don't mow half the yard, eat half an Oreo, or write half a . . .

But as far as the half of the Bible that we find in much of pop culture goes? It wouldn't be accurate to label it as the spoiled half of the apple or the flat half of the Coke. It's simply not complete, and that's okay. Don't write it off just because we don't get all the answers or because something isn't completely theologically correct. Or because it contains sinners acting like sinners. Don't write off pop culture because it doesn't give the answers that can only come from God and his message to us—the Bible.

Even the perfect, holy God was willing to save the city of Sodom from destruction if Abraham had found merely ten righteous people in all the land (Gen. 18:32). In what many call today's Sodom, are there not ten righteous people serving God with the talents he has given them? And concerning the rest of them, well, they're simply giving us half the Bible.

It's the church's job to provide the second half.

APPENDIX

The Real Noah and Moses Quiz

In 2014, Hollywood gave us two biblical blockbusters, *Noah* and *Exodus: Gods and Kings*. As with all "based on a true story" films, not all the details in the films were exactly right. Here are a few questions to test your knowledge on the biblical accounts found in the Old Testament books of Genesis and Exodus.

1. Which mountain did the ark rest on?
   a. Gerizim
   b. Gilboa
   c. Lebanon
   d. Ararat
   e. Kilamanjaro

2. Genesis alluded to a race of giants that existed before the Great Flood. What were they called?
   a. Nazarites
   b. Centaurs
   c. Troglodytes
   d. Nephilim
   e. Philistines

3. Although Noah's ark was measured in cubits, about how many feet long was it?
   a. 450
   b. 260
   c. 892
   d. 1660

4. According to Genesis 7, how long did the floodwaters cover the earth?

    a. 40 days and nights

    b. 100 days

    c. 360 days

    d. Just one weekend when they had planned a family picnic

    e. 150 days

5. What two birds did Noah use to measure the floodwaters?

    a. A sparrow and a raven

    b. A pterodactyl and a hummingbird

    c. A pigeon and a crow

    d. A hawk and a dove

    e. A raven and a dove

6. How old was Noah when the flood ended?

    a. 601 years

    b. 825 years

    c. 257 years

    d. 400 years

7. What did God tell Noah would be the sign of his covenant to never flood the earth again?

    a. The sunshine

    b. A secret handshake

    c. A rainbow

    d. The proliferation of animals

8. Which of Noah's sons was cursed for seeing his father's nakedness?

    a. Shem

    b. Ham

    c. Japeth

    d. Peeping Tom

    e. Canaan

9. What was the last of the ten plagues of Egypt?

    a. Locusts

    b. Death of the first born

    c. Darkness

    d. Excessive dandruff

10. What two plans did Pharaoh attempt to implement in order to begin destroying the Israelites?

    a. Drowning all the children; letting the sick die

    b. Having midwives kill all the babies born; working the older Israelites to death

    c. Throwing all the male children under age three into the Nile; threatening death to women who became pregnant

    d. Having the midwives kill all male children born; throwing all male babies into the Nile

11. How old was Moses when his mother put him in a basket and hid him among the reeds on the Nile?

    a. About fourteen years, just when he was starting to get a little obnoxious

    b. Three months

    c. Fourteen months

    d. Two weeks

12. When God called Moses from the burning bush, he told Moses that these people would listen to him.

    a. All of his people

    b. The new generations (youth)

    c. The angels of Heaven

    d. The elders and Pharaoh

13. Which of the following were NOT among the miracles God showed Moses at his calling? (three answers)

    a. A flaming sword

    b. A disease-like transformation of Moses' hand

    c. A vision of the Egyptian Moses killed

    d. A rod that became a serpent

    e. A dancing bear

14. Which of the following were among the plagues God brought on Egypt? (four answers)

    a. Frogs

    b. Blindness

    c. Leprosy

    d. Obvious tan lines

    e. Death of livestock

    f. Boils

    g. Lice

15. Which of the following did Moses take with him as the Israelites left Egypt?

    a. The body of Pharaoh's son

    b. The mummified body of Jacob

    c. His cell phone

    d. Blank tablets on which God would later inscribe the Ten Commandments

    e. The bones of Joseph

16. What did God do to the Egyptian army just prior to drowning them in the Red Sea?

    a. Forced them to eat brussels sprouts

    b. Took the wheels off their chariots

    c. Burned half of the army in a pillar of fire

    d. Caused many of the Egyptian soldiers to fall asleep

    e. Made their horses ill

17. Which of the following notable events happened at Mount Sinai?

    a. Jesus crucified

    b. Jesus asceneded

    c. Moses' first sinus attack

    d. Ten Commandments received

    e. Joshua defeats Moab

18. Why did Moses have his brother speak for him?

    a. Laryngitis

    b. He could do some neat sound effects.

    c. Exhaustion

    d. A lack of eloquence

19. What is the source of the Ten Commandments?

    a. God gave them to Noah.

    b. God gave them to Moses.

    c. Jesus gave them to us.

    d. They were first found in the ark of the covenant.

    e. Dr. Laura

20. What ruse did Moses' mother use to save him from being killed by the evil Pharaoh?

    a. She hid him in a manger in the stable.

    b. She hid him in a basket floating in the river.

    c. She sent him out of Egypt with a caravan of traders.

    d. She sent him to the Land of Nod.

    e. She turned him into a newt.

Answers: 1) d 2) d 3) a 4) e 5) e 6) a 7) c 8) b 9) b 10) d 11) b 12) d 13) a,c,e 14) a,e,f,g 15) e 16) b 17) d 18) d 19) b 20) b

NOTES

INTRODUCTION

1. "Domestic Grosses by MPAA Rating," Box Office Mojo, accessed November 6, 2014, http://www.boxofficemojo.com/alltime/domestic/mpaa.htm.

2. Dustin Rowles, "The 10 Highest Rated Cable Series of 2013," Warming Glow, December 16, 2013, http://uproxx.com/tv/2013/12/10-highest-rated-cables-series-2013/.

3. Frank E. Smitha, "Europe's Renaissance Begins," Macrohistory and World Timeline, accessed November 6, 2014, http://www.fsmitha.com/h3/renaissance.htm.

CHAPTER 1

1. *Superman Returns*, directed by Bryan Singer (Burbank, CA: Warner Home Video, Inc., 2006), DVD.

2. *The Avengers*, directed by Joss Whedon (Burbank, CA: Buena Vista Home Entertainment, Inc., 2012), DVD.

3. *Man of Steel*, directed by Jack Snyder (Burbank, CA: Warner Home Video, Inc., 2013), DVD.

4. Ibid.

5. *Spider-Man 2*, directed by Sam Raimi (Culver City, CA: Sony Pictures Home Entertainment, 2004), DVD.

6. Ibid.

7. *The Dark Knight*, directed by Christopher Nolan (Burbank, CA: Warner Home Video, Inc., 2008), DVD.

8. *Batman Begins*, directed by Christopher Nolan (Burbank, CA: Warner Home Video, Inc., 2005), DVD.

9. *The Dark Knight*, 2008.

10. Ibid.

11. *Thor*, directed by Kenneth Branagh (Hollywood, CA: Paramount Pictures, 2011), DVD.

CHAPTER 2

1. *Bruce Almighty*, directed by Tom Shadyac (Universal City, CA: Universal Studios Home Entertainment, 2003), DVD.

2. Ibid.

3. Ibid.

4. Ibid.

5. *Signs*, directed by M. Night Shyamalan, 2002 (Burbank, CA: Buena Vista Home Entertainment, 2003), DVD.

6. Ibid.

7. "*Signs*," Internet Movie Database, accessed November 6, 2014, http://www.imdb.com /title/tt0286106/?ref_=nv_sr_1.

8. *Signs*, 2003.

9. Ibid.

10. *The Book of Eli*, directed by the Hughes Brothers (Burbank, CA: Warner Home Video, 2010), DVD.

11. Ibid.

12. Ibid.

13. Ibid.

CHAPTER 3

1. *Despicable Me*, directed by Chris Renaud and Pierre Coffin (Universal City, CA: Universal Studios Home Entertainment, 2010), DVD.

2. Children's Bureau, "The 2013 AFCARS Report," National Foster Care Coalition, accessed November 6, 2014, http://www.nationalfostercare.org/latest-numbers-on -children-in-foster-care.html.

3. *The Croods*, directed by Chris Sanders and Kirk DeMicco (Beverly Hills, CA: Twentieth Century Fox Home Entertainment, 2013), DVD.

4. Ibid.

5. Ibid.

6. Ibid.

7. Ibid.

8. Ibid.

9. Ibid.

10. *Frozen*, directed by Chris Buck and Jennifer Lee, 2013 (Burbank, CA: Buena Vista Home Entertainment, 2014), DVD.

11. Ibid.

12. Ibid.

13. Ibid.

14. Ibid.

15. *The LEGO Movie*, directed by Phil Lord and Christopher Miller (Burbank, CA: Warner Home Video, 2014), DVD.

16. Ibid.

17. Ibid.

18. Ibid.

19. Ibid.

20. Ibid.

21. *Tangled*, directed by Nathan Greno and Byron Howard, 2010 (Burbank, CA: Buena Vista Home Entertainment, 2011), DVD.

22. *The Croods*, 2013.

23. *Despicable Me*, 2010.

24. Ibid.

CHAPTER 4

1. Mindy Kaling, "All My Problems Solved Forever . . ." *The Mindy Project*, season 2, episode 1, directed by Michael Spiller, aired September 17, 2013 (Universal City, CA: Universal Studios Home Entertainment, 2014), DVD.

2. Jack Burditt, "Triathlon," *The Mindy Project*, season 1, episode 22, directed by Wendey Stanzler, aired April 30, 2013 (Universal City, CA: Universal Studios Home Entertainment, 2013), DVD.

3. David Litt and Lee Aronsohn, "The Luminous Fish Effect," *The Big Bang Theory*, season 1, episode 4, directed by Mark Cendrowski, aired October 15, 2007 (Burbank, CA: Warner Home Video, 2008), DVD.

4. Ibid.

5. Bill Prady, Steven Molaro, and Jim Reynolds, "The Rhinitis Revelation," *The Big Bang Theory*, season 5, episode 6, directed by Howard Murray, aired October 20, 2011 (Burbank, CA: Warner Home Video, 2012), DVD.

6. Steven Molaro, "The Electric Can Opener Fluctuation," *The Big Bang Theory*, season 3, episode 1, directed by Mark Cendrowski, aired September 21, 2009 (Burbank, CA: Warner Home Vido, 2010), DVD.

7. Litt and Aronsohn, "The Luminous Fish Effect," *The Big Bang Theory*.

8. Joss Whedon, "Our Mrs. Reynolds," *Firefly*, directed by Vondie Curtis-Hall, aired on October 4, 2002 (Beverly Hills, CA: Twentieth Century Fox Home Entertainment, 2003), DVD.

9. Tim Minear, "Bushwhacked," *Firefly*, directed by Tim Minear, aired on September 27, 2002 (Beverly Hills, CA: Twentieth Century Fox Home Entertainment, 2003), DVD.

10. Cheryl Cain, "War Stories," *Firefly*, directed by James A. Contner, aired on December 6, 2002 (Beverly Hills, CA: Twentieth Century Fox Home Entertainment, 2003), DVD.

11. Joss Whedon and Tim Minear, "The Train Job," *Firefly*, directed by Joss Whedon, aired on September 27, 2002 (Beverly Hills, CA: Twentieth Century Fox Home Entertainment, 2003), DVD.

12. Ben Edlund, "Jaynestown," *Firefly*, directed by Marita Grabiak, aired on October 18, 2002 (Beverly Hills, CA: Twentieth Century Fox Home Entertainment, 2003), DVD.

13. *Serenity*, directed by Joss Whedon, 2005 (Universal City, CA: Universal Studios Home Entertainment, 2006), DVD.

14. *Saved!*, directed by Brian Dannelly (Los Angeles, CA: MGM/UA Home Video, 2004), DVD.

15. Ibid.

16. Ibid.

17. Ibid.

18. *Beautiful Creatures*, directed by Richard LaGravenese (Burbank, CA: Warner Home Video, 2013), DVD.

19. Tim Long, "The Devil Wears Nada," *The Simpsons*, season 21, episode 5, directed by Nancy Kruse and Mike B. Anderson, aired November 15, 2009 (Beverly Hills, CA: Twentieth Century Fox Home Entertainment, 2010).

20. Jeff Martin, "Homer's Barbershop Quartet," *The Simpsons*, season 5, episode 1, directed by Mark Kirkland, aired September 30, 1993 (Beverly Hills, CA: Twentieth Century Fox Home Entertainment, 1994).

21. Jeff Martin, "Dead Putting Society," *The Simpsons*, season 2, episode 6, directed by Rich Moore, aired November 15, 1990 (Beverly Hills, CA: Twentieth Century Fox Home Entertainment, 1991).

CHAPTER 5

1. Chris Seay, *The Gospel According to Lost* (Nashville: Thomas Nelson, 2009).

2. Damon Lindelof and Drew Goddard, "Flashes Before Your Eyes," *Lost*, season 3, episode 8, directed by Jack Bender, aired February 14, 2007 (Burbank, CA: Buena Vista Home Entertainment, 2007).

3. Ibid.

4. Carlton Cuse and Damon Lindelof, "The Constant," *Lost*, season 4, episode 5, directed by Jack Bender, aired February 28, 2008 (Burbank, CA: Buena Vista Home Entertainment, 2008).

5. Edward Kitsis, Adam Horowitz, and Elizabeth Sarnoff, "What They Died For," *Lost*, season 6, episode 16, directed by Paul Edwards, aired May 18, 2010 (Burbank, CA: Buena Vista Home Entertainment, 2010).

6. Ibid.

7. Carlton Cuse and Damon Lindelof, "Lighthouse," *Lost*, season 6, episode 5, directed by Jack Bender, aired February 23, 2010 (Burbank, CA: Buena Vista Home Entertainment, 2010).

8. Damon Lindelof and Carlton Cuse, "316," *Lost*, season 5, episode 6, directed by Stephen Williams, aired February 18, 2009 (Burbank, CA: Buena Vista Home Entertainment, 2009).

9. Melinda Hsu Taylor and Greggory Nations, "Ab Aeterno," *Lost*, season 6, episode 9, directed by Tucker Gates, aired March 23, 2010 (Burbank, CA: Buena Vista Home Entertainment, 2010).

10. Lindelof and Cuse, "316."

11. Ibid.

12. Carlton Cuse and Damon Lindelof, "The 23rd Psalm," *Lost*, season 2, episode 10, directed by Matt Earl Beesley, aired January 11, 2006 (Burbank, CA: Buena Vista Home Entertainment, 2006).

13. Edward Kitsis and Adam Horowitz, "Dr. Linus," *Lost*, season 6, episode 7, directed by Mario Van Peebles, aired March 9, 2010 (Burbank, CA: Buena Vista Home Entertainment, 2010).

14. Damon Lindelof and Carlton Cuse, "There's No Place Like Home, Part 1," *Lost*, season 4, episode 12, directed by Stephen Williams, aired May 15, 2008 (Burbank, CA: Buena Vista Home Entertainment, 2008).

15. Kitsis and Horowitz, "Dr. Linus."

16. Taylor and Nations, "Ab Aeterno."

17. Damon Lindelof and Carlton Cuse, "The End," *Lost*, season 6, episode 17, directed by Jack Bender, aired May 23, 2010 (Burbank, CA: Buena Vista Home Entertainment, 2010).

18. "The 15 Biggest Bestsellers EVER After the Bible," *Huffington Post*, July 30, 2010, http://www.huffingtonpost.com/2010/07/30/the-15-biggest-bestseller_n_664029 .html#s115965title=Quotations_from_Chairman.

CHAPTER 6

1. *Fixer Upper*, "Nomadic Suburbanites Seek Unique Retro Residence," HGTV, aired May 1, 2014.

2. *Undercover Boss*, "ADT," CBS, aired April 12, 2013.

3. *Extreme Makeover: Home Edition*, "Slaughter Family, ABC, aired January 3, 2009.

4. *Extreme Makeover: Home Edition*, "Gaudet Family," ABC, aired March 23, 2008.

5. *Who Do You Think You Are?* "Rachel McAdams," TLC, aired August 6, 2014.

CHAPTER 7

1. *Oprah Prime*, on the Oprah Winfrey Network, April 14, 2014.

2. "John Legend—All of Me Lyrics," SongLyrics.com, accessed November 6, 2014, http://www.songlyrics.com/john-legend/all-of-me-lyrics/.

3. "Relaxing Spa Music Long Time," YouTube, video posted by maulanababaji, April 21, 2012, accessed November 6, 2014, https://www.youtube.com/watch?v=Kgh7IJ8yqX8.

4. Christina Perri, *Head or Heart*, Atlantic Records, 2014, inside cover.

5. "Imagine Dragons—Bleeding Out," SongMeanings.com, accessed November 6, 2014, http://songmeanings.com/songs/view/3530822107859439841/.

CHAPTER 8

1. *Rocky IV*, directed by Sylvester Stallone, 1985 (Beverly Hills, CA: Twentieth Century Fox Home Entertainment, 2005), DVD.

2. "Author Unknown," QuoteWorld.org, accessed November 6, 2014, http://quoteworld.org/quotes/10823.[1]

3. "Jay Leno Quotes," ThinkExist.com, accessed November 6, 2014, http://thinkexist.com/quotation/if_god_doesn-t_destroy_hollywood_boulevard-he/198489.html[2].

AFTERWORD

1. J. K. Rowling, *Harry Potter and the Deathly Hollows* (New York: Scholastic, 2007), 712.

2. *The Fault in Our Stars*, directed by Josh Boone. (Released June 6, 2014, by Twentieth Century Fox).

ACKNOWLEDGMENTS

Dedicating the book to my wife, Amy, isn't nearly enough. Her support and help with this book began many years before the book itself even began. When we met in college, she had never watched an episode of *Seinfeld* or even seen *Star Wars*. (What?!) And if anyone has *Real Genius* on DVD, could I please borrow it? She pretty much danced her way through the '80s and can only remember watching *E.T.* and *On Golden Pond*. But twenty years later, she has seen hundreds of movies by my side and gets teary-eyed when our favorite TV shows, like *Lost*, *Psych*, and *The Office* go off the air. But beyond her support of my love for pop culture, more importantly she threw herself "all in" when she married this English major who never wanted to work in an office but only wanted to work somehow with the creativity God had given him. Through both bad decisions and great ones, somehow we have made it this far, Amy!

I have worked at home every single day of my kids' lives, so when I told them that during this writing project I would have to spend more evenings and weekends working away from them than normal, I think that hurt me more than it did them. But they were totally cool with everything and did an amazing job at keeping it (fairly) quiet around the house. (Though the noise-cancelling headphones were still a great investment.) MacKenna, thanks for watching some of the princess movies with me. It was weird watching *Cinderella* by myself. Camden, I love our superhero movie days when I pick you up early from school because we just can't wait until that night to see it. I hope you keep the same priorities with your children.

Thank you, also, to our friend and old neighbor Samantha, who gave us all her princess movies when she thought our daughter was old enough to enjoy them. I didn't have to spend a single dollar on all that research.

Thanks to Aaron Earls for pointing me toward *The Mindy Project*. For many hours I put on my headphones at my desk and laughed and laughed. Who knows what my family was thinking while hearing all that. And your help with me getting my history straight was invaluable. You're my new go-to reference on everything. And thanks also for getting me addicted to our family's new favorite show, *Doctor Who*. If there's ever a sequel to this book, the Doctor will have to be in it somehow.

To my editor, Alee Anderson, do you remember the time years ago when I told you your name sounded like that of a superhero's girlfriend? Turns out I was wrong. It's you who is the superhero. I don't know what I did to get in your good graces, but please don't ever leave the publishing industry. Where you go, I go. That's how important you have become to me and my family.

Judith, you made me both a better writer and a better editor. Thanks for your honest feedback and helpful edits.

There are too many people to list who I sincerely want to thank for giving someone like me a chance to begin proofreading in the publishing industry over a decade ago. I will be eternally grateful to each of you for being such huge parts in this journey of mine.

It may sound cliché, but it's 100 percent authentic: Thank you, God, for everything you have done in my life. We broke all the publishing rules: no agent, no social media platform, no book proposal, no problem. I had you.

ABOUT THE AUTHOR

Kevin Harvey has spent the last twelve years doing anything and everything he could to work in the Christian publishing industry, and will continue to do so when the excitement of this book dies down. He also has a self-published book, *Jonah, John, and the Second Greatest (but Most Avoided) Commandment*, that he would love to shorten the title of someday. Copies can still be found on Amazon, as well as in his attic.

Kevin lives in the perfectly sized town of Wake Forest, North Carolina, with his wife, Amy, and his two children, Camden and MacKenna, where he also coaches youth baseball and serves in a church plant. He is currently attempting to have a vaguely active social media presence. You can follow him on Twitter at @GodFamilyNoles, as well as read more of his observations concerning the Bible in pop culture at www.bibleinpopculture.com.

LEARN *Even* MORE ABOUT

POP CULTURE'S

FAVORITE BOOK

WORD SEARCHES, & MAZES, GAMES, CROSSWORD PUZZLES

QUEEN'S CARAVAN

For the Queen of Sheba, seeing was believing, and until she saw for herself, she couldn't quite believe the rumors of the wealth and wisdom of King Solomon. So she and her retinue made a great journey of over 1,000 miles from southwest Arabia (what is now Yemen) to Jerusalem, to "test him with hard questions."

First Kings 10:4–5 says, "When the queen of Sheba had seen all the wisdom of Solomon, the house that he had built, the food on his table, the seating of his servants, the service of his waiters and their apparel, his cupbearers, and his entryway by which he went up to the house of the LORD, there was no more spirit in her." She was overwhelmed. The stories she had heard about Solomon were no exaggeration, for she said, "Indeed, the half was not told me."

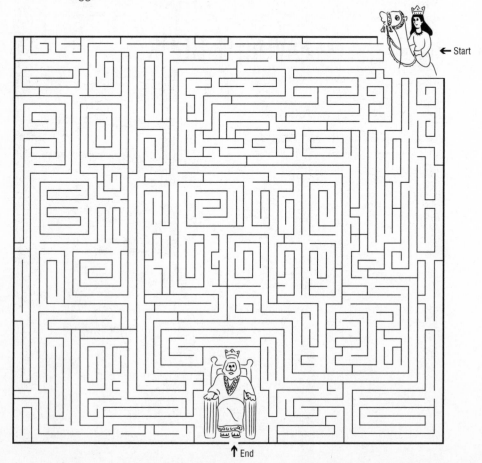

← Start

↑ End

CROSSWORD PUZZLE

Continued on following pages.

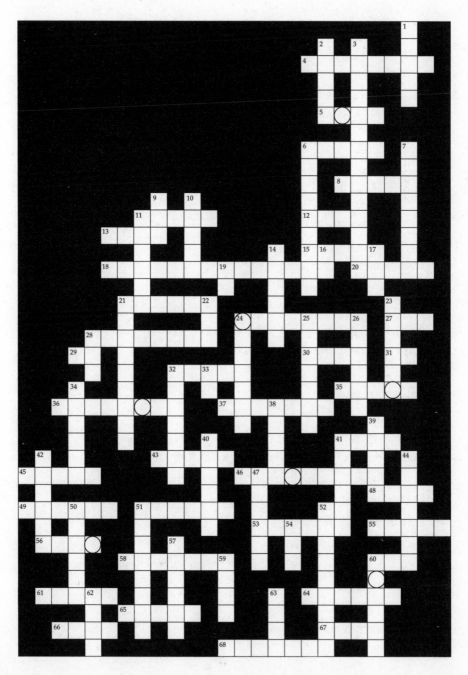

Across

4 Solomon's successor; ten tribes revolted against him

5 Son of Eve, father of Enosh

6 "Brother of the Lord" who led early Jerusalem church

8 Canaanite king he reigned In Hazor, oppressed Israel

11 One of Isaac's sons

12 #2 Down preached, "You are the ___ of the earth."

13 Skilled in driving tent pegs, she defeated Sisera

15 #2 Down said, "Assuredly, I say to you, inasmuch as you did it to one of the ___ of these My brethren, you did it to Me" (NKJ).

18 Gospel writer (3 words)

20 Shechem tried to enter into ___ with #11 Across (Genesis 34:8–10).

21 Earthly father of Jesus

24 Son of Saul, friend to David

27 Mother of all

28 He led tribes in rebellion, followers into idolatry

29 #2 Down taught, "Whatever you want men to ___ to you, ___ also to them, for this is the Law and the Prophets" (NKJ).

30 Wise men came from the ___ to worship #2 Down.

31 "God ___ love."

32 City at the southern limits of tribe of #45 Across

35 In list of "sons of Solomon's servants"

36 Mother of Miriam, Aaron, and Moses

37 Descendants of Abraham, later known as #25 Down

41 Son of Pethuel, author of a minor prophetic book

43 Thessalonican believer hospitable to Paul and Silas

45 Fourth son of #11 Across

46 Persons who lived near Jebus

48 As #3 Down cried in the wilderness, his words may have been heard as an ___ in the hills.

49 One of the sons of Tola

51 King at eight years old, he ruled for thirty-one years with great integrity.

52 #2 Down said, "Where your treasure is, there your heart will ____ also" (NKJ).

53 One of the twelve precious stones in the priest's breastplate

55 Region settled by descendants of Japheth

56 #2 Down said, "If you ____ faith as a mustard seed" (NKJ).

58 Ahab's wicked wife

60 Contraction for Jehovah (Psalm 68:4)

61 One of seven men in 1 Chronicles 5:13

64 One of daughters of #28 Down

65 Disciples of #2 Down asked, "Who then can be ____?"

66 Husband of #58 Across

67 Book that opens with a prophecy by #51 Down

68 Son of Jeshua

Down

1 Gideon's father

2 King of kings

3 Preacher in Judean wilderness (3 words)

6 #2 Down wept over this city

7 Title of #2 Down (3 words)

9 Another word for friend

10 Fish food, temporarily

11 Fatherinlaw of Moses, priest of Midian

14 Wife of officer in Herod's housebold

16 Short for editor

17 In one of his letters, #18 Across said we must always "____ the spirits."

19 #2 Down said, "____ their fruits you will know them" (NKJ).

21 One of Hezron's sons

22 Youngest son of Noah

23 One of the sons of Tola

24 A city and plain, battlefield where Gideon won

25 Literally, descendants of Judah

26 Brother of Joel, one of King David's valiant men

28   He suffered, temporarily

32   Mother of #51 Across

33   #2 Down's final command in Matthew 28:19 begins with this word.

34   Israelite leader after Moses

38   Helped spies escape from her home city, Jericho

39   Father of eight sons, of whom David was youngest

40   River connecting Sea of Galilee and Dead Sea

41   Gideon's firstborn son

42   One of Esau's wives, daughter of Beeri the Hittite

44   Name used for God, literally means "self-subsisting"

47   Many thought #3 Down was this Old Testament prophet

50   #2 Down is called the _____ by #18 Across

51   Considered one of four great Old Testament prophets

52   City where #2 Down was born

54   #34 Down was part of a group sent by Moses to _____ out the land.

57   Firstborn son of #11 Across

59   The nature of #60 Across is _____

60   One of Asher's sons

62   #2 Down is called the "last _____"

63   One of Onam's sons

Bonus "J"

Write down the letters that are circled in the crossword grid. Unscramble them to form yet another "J" word.

___ ___ ___ ___ ___ ___ ___

JONAH'S JOURNEY

Although the book of Jonah, particulary Jonah's encounter with the great fish, has been viewed with skepticism by unbelievers, Jesus vouched for its truth in Matthew 12:39–41.

Jonah, a native of Galilee, was one of the earlier prophets. He is sometimes called the "reluctant missionary" since he was largely unwilling to answer God's call to go to Nineveh and warn the enemies of his country of God's coming judgment.

Jonah was a mixture of strength and weakness. Obviously a convincing orator, he was something of a whiner who was more concerned with his own reputation than with what God commanded. One of the curious facts of this story is that Jonah was disappointed that the Ninevites repented! (See Johah 3:4–4:1.)

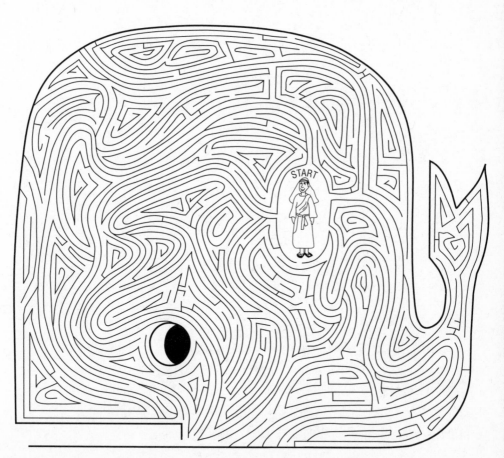

SAFARI TIME!

Find the names of 37 different animals mentioned in the Bible in the square below.

```
O   Z   D   R   A   Z   I   L   E   L   I   Z   A   M   E
X   D   R   A   G   O   N   T   L   E   L   H   B   E   L
E   E   N   I   W   S   L   Y   E   M   I   C   E   T   G
N   E   L   U   A   E   I   M   P   A   U   O   H   S   A
Y   R   M   G   O   D   O   Z   H   C   B   L   E   G   E
X   T   E   P   L   H   N   C   A   A   A   U   M   R   E
L   L   A   M   B   O   Y   A   N   P   T   T   O   A   H
U   R   U   R   E   R   M   E   T   E   N   Z   T   F   A
D   L   C   S   A   S   S   E   R   Z   E   K   H   L   R
E   C   M   A   R   E   T   A   O   G   P   C   R   E   E
D   H   U   S   L   B   F   X   M   A   R   O   L   S   F
E   A   R   A   O   F   A   L   F   O   E   L   L   A   I
R   C   H   A   M   E   L   E   O   N   S   L   A   E   E
S   W   R   N   V   M   L   I   X   W   T   U   C   W   H
H   P   S   P   E   E   H   S   O   L   I   B   U   L   C
E   N   R   O   C   I   N   U   N   O   N   L   L   O   L
```

WORD POOL

APE ASS BEAR BEHEMOTH BOAR BULLOCK CALF CAMEL CATTLE
CHAMELEON DEER DRAGON EAGLE ELEPHANT FOX GOAT
GREYHOUND HARE HEIFER HORSE LAMB LEOPARD LION LIZARD
MICE MULE OXEN RAM RAVEN ROE SERPENT SHEEP SWINE
UNICORN WEASEL WHALE WOLF

AS WHITE AS SNOW

Although snow in the Middle East lands of the Bible is rare, it is mentioned in Scripture. It is called the "treasury of snow" in the book of Job (38:22), and it is under God's control, "For He says to the snow, 'Fall on the earth'" (37:6).

Most often, snow is used to describe moral purity and righteousness. On the Mt. of Transfiguration, Jesus' clothes were described as "shining, exceedingly white, like snow, such as no launderer on earth can whiten them" (Mark 9:3). But perhaps the most precious and familiar verse on snow is the promise contained in Isaiah 1 :18: "Though your sins are like scarlet, they shall be as white as snow."

LOTS OF CIRCLES

Every school child knows that there was a time before Columbus when people thought the earth was flat. But had those people had access to the Scripture and read Isaiah 40:22, all doubt about the earth's shape would have been erased. "It is He who sits above the circle of the earth," it says (emphasis added). Did you ever wonder what wide knowledge of the Scripture might have meant to world history?

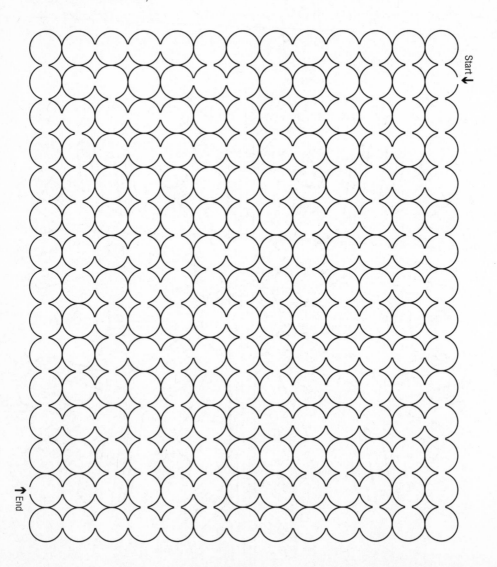

Start ↓

↑ End

NOAH QUIZ

Try to to solve this equation without consulting the story of Noah and the Great Flood (Genesis 5:32–9:29).

The number of every clean animal that
God told Noah to take into the ark   _____

The number of every unclean animal that
God told Noah to take into the ark   ✕   _____

The number of the month in which the
rain began to fall   ✕   _____

The day of the month that the rain began
to fall   ✕   _____

The number of days that "the waters
prevailed upon the earth"   +   _____

The number of days and nights that the
rain fell on the earth   —   _____

The number of the month when the tops
of the mountains could be seen   +   _____

The number of Noah's sons   +   _____

The number of times Noah sent out birds
to see how dry the earth had become   +   _____

The number of decks in the ark   —   _____

Noah's age when he entered the ark   =   _____

EARTH, SKY AND SEA

. . . what more is there?

Clue: MESSIAH is SKYYOGN

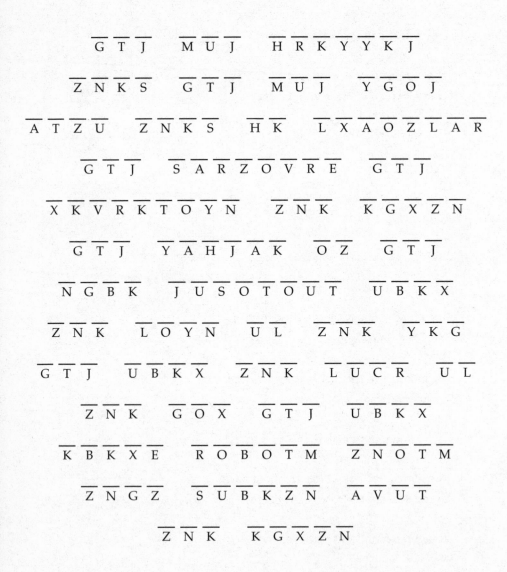

GTJ MUJ HRKYYKJ

ZNKS GTJ MUJ YGOJ

ATZU ZNKS HK LXAOZLAR

GTJ SARZOVRE GTJ

XKVRKTOYN ZNK KGXZN

GTJ YAHJAK OZ GTJ

NGBK JUSOTOUT UBKX

ZNK LOYN UL ZNK YKG

GTJ UBKX ZNK LUCR UL

ZNK GOX GTJ UBKX

KBKXE ROBOTM ZNOTM

ZNGZ SUBKZN AVUT

ZNK KGXZN

REVELATION

Most of the answers to these clues are found in the Book of Revelation although the clue may not refer to its usage there. *Continued on following page.*

Across

1 Remains when light is gone

7 Drink made from leaves

9 Sugary

11 Splendor

13 Sufficiently skilled

14 Frog relative

15 Each (abbr.)

16 Affirmative

17 Man's name

19 Lord's prayer—first word

20 Limited (abbr.)

22 Female deer

23 The New City

26 Astonishing, spectacular

29 Flexible, resilient

32 Memo or jotting

33 Mother or father

35 Suffix meaning more

36 Two words to wed

37 Beelzebub

38 Annoy, nettle

39 Satan's garden persona

41 Resting place

44 Jewish homeland

45 Have debt

46 Fifth note of the scale

47 Feeble

48 Island of revelation

Down

1 Mythical reptile; Satan

2 Sovereign

3 Property, land

4 Weapon; Bible

5 Stamp, imprint

6 Era

7 Endeavor

8 Window of the soul

10 Edward's nickname

12 John saw seven; candleholders

17 Vapor, haze

18 One who swears

21 Blemish, stain

23 Precious stone, first foundation of
    New Jerusalem

24 Ample, great

25 Abraham's nephew

26 Exalt, revere

27 Bird's homemaking

28 God's promissory note

30 Flower necklace

31 Rock

34 First boat of note

38 Notion

40 Betrayal signal

42 Female sheep

43 Sitting place for child

JUDGES

We all know the story of the Old Testament heavyweight and the woman who belied the term "weaker sex." Samson's love for Delilah turned out to be misplaced, but his love for God brought him victory against all odds. Before you refer to Judges 13–16 in the New King James Bible, see how many details of this story you can recall. *Continued on following pages.*

Across

2 Lacking license plates, this was Samson's jailhouse occupation.

5 Samson could have written a book entitled "The Secret of My ____ ."

6 In the end, Samson had to do it. (But he had company.)

8 How many bowstrings did Delilah tie on Samson?

9 These "windows" were closed.

13 This wedding vow verb led to Samson's downfall.

14 With the batten of this, Delilah wove Samson's tresses.

18 Samson's father placed his offering on this.

19 Samson was one of these from the womb.

20 Samson's was tangled before he came clean.

22 The "edge" of Samson's night

24 Samson's father made this type of offering.

27 Hometown of Samson's father

28 Samson mocked Delilah with one of these—three times.

29 How many years Samson determined right and wrong in Israel

31 Delilah's reward would be ____ hundred pieces of silver from each Philistine ruler.

32 Samson could spin one, but it had no power to hold him.

34 These fetters would come in third at the Games

36 Samson brought this house down.

37 A less-than-gilded cage

Down

1 This potable never touched Samson's lips

3 The Philistines' god

4 Samson brought in the verdict

7 Samson carried the gateposts of this city to a hilltop facing Hebron. (This happened before he met Delilah.)

8 Delilah chose not to go for the gold.

10 Down in this valley, Samson met Delilah.

11 Samson's mother had to avoid food that wasn't spotless, just as any sacrifice offered to God could not be this.

12 Seven locks were Samson's key.

15 As long as he avoided barbers, Samson's power switch was in this position.

16 Samson's father

17 Samson tore one apart as if it were a young goat.

21 Samson's mother shared this condition with Abraham's wife, Sarah.

23 Column A and Column B

25 New or used, these weren't the ties that bound Samson.

26 How many thousand men and women died after Samson's last performance.

30 Interlace

33 It wasn't safe for Samson to take one of these with Delilah around

35 This one told no tails after the fire.

In the circled letters you will find God's promised provision for you to overcome temptation—*if you look for it!*

— —— ——   —— ——   —— —— —— —— —— ——

ICHTHUS

The sign of the fish came into use as a symbol of Christ in the second century. The symbol may have derived from the acrostic IXOYE (the Greek word for fish), with the letters standing for Jesus Christ, Son of God, Savior. Or the acrostic may have come from the symbol.

The fish is sometimes used as a symbol of baptism. Tertullian writes of new Christians as being little fishes following the Fish in the second birth that occurs in the waters of baptism.

The fish is sometimes a symbol of the Eucharist. Catacomb paintings of the fourth and fifth centuries frequently include the fish symbol in combination with bread and wine.

From early times, fish—especially dried fish—took the place of meat on days of fasting. The symbol of the fish is thus sometimes associated with the separation of Christians from the world.

In recent times individuals and organizations have used the fish symbol to testify to their identification with Christ.

Start

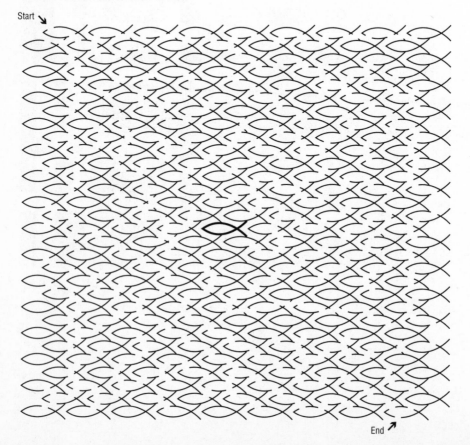

End

THE PSALMS

The Psalms were written centuries ago, but the emotions they express are as current as our times. As we read through this book, we find ourselves caught up in the celebrations and heartaches of the writers—the times when God convincingly trounced the enemy, as well as those dark nights of the soul when God seemed very far away. Fill in as many answers as you can before consulting the chapter and verse given at the end of each clue. Refer to the New King James Bible. *Continued on following pages.*

Across

5 "____ is he who has the God of Jacob for his help" (146:5).

7 In front of the wicked, David was mute with silence. He held his peace, even from good, and his ____ was stirred up (39:2).

8 "Trouble and ____ have overtaken me, yet Your commandments are my delights" (119:143).

11 Physician (abbr.)

13 David said that God had heard his vows, and had given him the _____ of those who #2 Down His name (61:5).

15 David asked God not to rebuke him in His #24 Down, "nor chasten me in Your hot _____" (6:1).

19 When the terrors of death had fallen upon him, and fearfulness and trembling, and horror had overwhelmed him, David longed for the wings of a _____ , to fly away and be at rest (55:4–6).

20 "I see the treacherous, and am _____ , because they do not keep Your word" (119:158).

22 Keep my soul, and deliver me; let me not be _____ , for I put my trust in You (25:20).

24 The foundations of the hills quaked and were shaken, because He was _____ (18:7).

25 "Why does Your #24 Down _____ against the sheep of Your pasture?" (74:1)

26 A nurse's initials

28 Should David's enemies "escape by iniquity?" In #24 Down cast down the _____ , O God!" (sing.) (56:7)

29 The man who avoids the ungodly, sinners, and the scornful finds _____ in the #27 Down of the Lord (1:1.2).

31 "Turn Yourself to me, and have mercy on me, for I am _____ and afflicted" (25:16)

34 The #36 Down and the deceitful fought against David without a cause. In return for his _____ , they were his accusers. But he gave himself to prayer (109:2–4).

35 "My flesh trembles for #2 Down of You, and I am afraid of Your _____" (119:120).

36 "For they persecute the ones You have struck, and talk of the #9 Down of those You have _____" (69:26).

38 Mountains with more than one _____ fumed with #17 Down because God chose to dwell in the mountain of Bashan forever (68:16).

39 David moaned noisily because of the enemy and the oppression of the #36 Down. "For they bring down trouble upon me, and in _____ they #23 Down me" (55:2, 3).

40 "Lord, all my _____ is before You; and my sighing is not hidden from You" (38:9).

41 The Israelites provoked God to #24 Down with their high places, and moved Him to _____ with their carved images (78:58).

42 The fate that David wished for God's enemies: "Let them be confounded and _____ forever; yes, let them be put to #1 Down and perish," that they might know God is the Most High over all the earth (83:17).

Down

1 "Because for Your sake I have borne reproach; _____ has covered my face" (69:7).

2 "The secret of the LORD is with those who _____ Him, and He will show them His covenant" (25:14).

3 The workers of iniquity are in great #2 Down, for God has scattered the _____ of him who encamps against God's people (53:5).

4 "In Your presence is fullness of _____" (16:11).

6 When the #36 Down sees the honor heaped upon the #26 Down man, he will be _____; he will gnash his teeth and melt away (112:10).

9 David said his eye "wastes away" because of this; his eye grows old because of all his enemies (6:7).

10 "You #34 Across all _____ words, you deceitful tongue," David said, referring to the man who boasts in evil (52:4).

11 "Why are you _____, O my soul? And why are you disquieted within me? Hope in God." (Two words, reverse order) (43:5).

12 Asking God to protect, or save, David said," _____ my life from #2 Down of the enemy" (64:1).

14 "Arise, O LORD, in Your #24 Down; lift Yourself up because of the _____ of my enemies" (7:6).

16 "As a father his children, so the Lord _____ those who #2 Down Him" (103:13).

17 When this emotion was felt against Moses and Aaron, the earth opened up and swallowed Dathan, and covered the faction of Abiram. A fire burned up the #36 Down (106:16–18).

18 God's people will #2 Down Him as long as the ____ and moon endure (72:5).

21 If he could have flown like a bird, David could have fled the terrors of death and the fearfulness, trembling, and horror that overwhelmed him. He could have escaped from the windy storm and ____ (55:4–8).

23 What right do the #36 Down have to declare God's statutes? They ____ instruction and they cast God's words behind them (50:16, 17).

24 "There is no soundness in my flesh because of Your ____, nor any health in my #3 Down because of my sin" (38:3).

26 The man who boasts in evil will be destroyed by God forever. The ____ also shall see and #2 Down and laugh, saying, "Here is the man who did not make God his strength" (52:5–7).

27 "I #23 Down the double-minded, but I #34 Across Your ____" (119:113).

28 "Make vows to the LORD your God and pay them; let all who are around Him bring ____ to Him who ought to be feared" (76:11).

30 "When you eat the labor of your ____, you shall be #5 Across, and it shall be well with you" (sing.) (128:2).

31 "Let me not sink; let me be ____ from those who #23 Down me, and out of the deep waters" (69:14)

32 "The #2 Down of the LORD is the beginning of ____" (111:10).

33 "Come and bear, all you who #2 Down God, and I will declare what He has done for my ____" (66:16).

35 "Let the heavens rejoice . . . let the field be ____, and all that is in it. Then all the trees of the woods will rejoice before the LORD" (96:11, 12).

36 When Asaph saw the prosperity of the ____, he was envious. But then he saw that God set them "in slippery places. . . . Oh, how they are brought to desolation, as in a moment! They are utterly consumed with terrors" (73:18.19).

37 Because God was his shield, David said, "I will not be ____ of ten thousands of #28 Across who have set themselves against me all around. . . . Salvation belongs to the LORD" (3:6, 8).

PROVERBS

Words to the would-be wise! *Continued on following pages.*

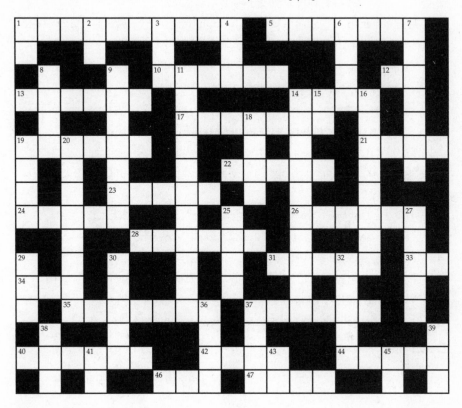

Across

1 "A _____ turns away wrath" (2 words) (Proverbs 15:1).

5 "A _____ does not love one who corrects him" (Proverbs 15:12).

10 "Fools despise _____ and instruction" (Proverbs 1:7).

12 "Train _____ a child in the way he should go" (Proverbs 22:6).

13 A virtuous wife is worth "far above _____" (Proverbs 31:10).

14 "Like one who takes away a garment in _____ weather . . . is one who sings songs to a heavy heart" (Proverbs 25:20).

17 Proverbs of _____ .

19 "_____ is a little with the fear of Lord, than great treasure with trouble" (Proverbs 15:16).

21 "Let your eyes _____ straight ahead" (Proverbs 4:25).

22 "Keep your ___ with all diligence" (Proverbs 4:23).

23 One of six things the Lord hates: "a ___ look" (Proverbs 6:17).

24 "___ in the Lord with all your heart" (Proverbs 3:5).

26 "It is easier for a ___ [pl.] to go through the eye of a needle than for rich man to enter the kingdom of God" (Matthew 19:24).

28 "Like one who binds ___ ___ in a sling is he who gives honor to a fool" (2 words) (Proverbs 26:8).

31 "For the commandment is a lamp, and the law a ___ " (Proverbs 6:23).

33 "___ for the upright, he establishes his way" (Proverbs 21:29).

34 "Do not ___ the bread of a miser" (Proverbs 23:6).

35 Three too-wonderful things: "the way of a ___ on a rock" (Proverbs 30:18–19).

37 "The ___ of the righteous is choice silver" (Proverbs 10:20).

40 "Let her own works ___ her in the gates" (Proverbs 31:31).

42 "For the ___ gives wisdom" (Proverbs 2:6).

44 Riches sometimes "fly away like an ___" (Proverbs 23:5).

46 "The LORD is the maker of them ___ " (Proverbs 22:2).

47 "___ who go to her [evil] return" (Proverbs 2:19).

Down

1 "As iron sharpens iron, ___ a man sharpens the countenance of his friend" (Proverbs 27:17).

2 "Go ___ the ant, you sluggard!" (Proverbs 6:6).

3 Worthless persons . . . "___ [pl.] discord" (Proverbs 6:12, 14).

4 "He who spares his ___ hates his son" (Proverbs 13:24).

6 "A ___ rages and is self-confident" (Proverbs 14:16).

7 "He that regardeth ___ is prudent" (Proverbs 15:5, KJV).

8 "By me [wisdom] princes ___" (Proverbs 8:16).

9 Proof of payment made

11 "Fools despise wisdom and ___" (Proverbs 1:7).

14 "Do not despise the chastening of the LORD, nor detest His ___" (Proverbs 3:11).

15 "He who rolls a stone will have it roll back ___ him" (Proverbs 26:27).

16 "The hand of the ___ makes rich" (Proverbs 10:4).

18 "Where no ___ are, the trough is clean" (Proverbs 14:4).

19 "Earnestly desire the ___ gifts" (1 Corinthians 12:31).

20 "The ___ of the wicked are an abomination to the LORD" (Proverbs 15:26).

25 "The desire of the righteous is ___ good" (Proverbs 11:23).

27 "He who has a ___ hand becomes poor" (Proverbs 10:4).

29 "Will you ___ your eyes on that which is not?" (Proverbs 23:5).

30 "Wisdom . . . speaks her ___" (Proverbs 1:20–21).

32 "Seldom set foot in your neighbor's ___" (Proverbs 25:17).

36 "Ask . . . the birds of the air, and they will ___ you" (Job 12:7).

37 "Wise men ___ away wrath" (Proverbs 29:8).

38 To fail to heed God's proverbs

39 "Do not ___ your heart be glad when he [your enemy] stumbles" (Proverbs 24:17).

41 "Deceit is ___ the heart of those who devise evil" (Proverbs 12:20).

43 "___ you see a man hasty in his words? There is more hope for a fool than for him" (Proverbs 29:20).

45 "Do not ___ hastily to court" (Proverbs 25:8).

GIANT VS. SHEPHERD

The young shepherd David was dwarfed by the Philistine giant Goliath who stood six cubits and a span (over nine feet tall). Heavily armed, Goliath jeered his enemy's choice of David to battle with him in a showdown between Philistia and Israel in the valley of Elah.

It wasn't exactly that David was the Israelites' choice, it was more that David was the only willing volunteer. In fact, David was insulted at Goliath's challenge, and he asked, "Who is this uncircumcised Philistine, that he should defy the armies of the living God?" (1 Samuel 17:26).

What were David's fighting credentials? He told King Saul that he had slain a lion and a bear when they came after his flock of sheep. "This uncircumcised Philistine will be like one of them," (v. 36) he told Saul, convincing the king to let him go to battle for the army of Israel.

Besides having the tactical advantage of the long-range slingshot, David claimed the Lord gave him another advantage: "The LORD does not save with sword and spear; for the battle is the LORD's" (v. 47). After the stone flew out of David's sling, knocking Goliath to the ground, David ran over to the Philistine, drew Goliath's sword from its sheath, and cut off the giant's head.

Help David gather five stones for his battle against Goliath. Do not cross over a path that has already been used.

SAFE PASSAGE

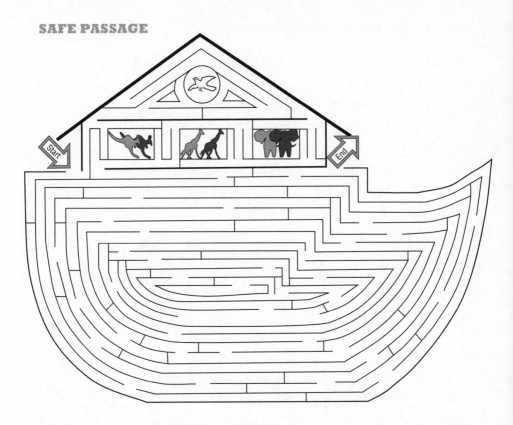

Genesis 6:14–9:17 gives us a remarkable account of a man's faith in God in the face of seemingly ridiculous instructions. Not only did God tell Noah that it was going to rain (a phenomenon heretofore unknown), but that he was to save himself, his family, and a pair of every animal species by building a huge boat.

God was very specific about how the ark was to be built giving specific materials (gopherwood and pitch), size (450 feet long, seventy-five feet wide, and forty-five feet high), and arrangement (three decks, a door in the side with a window). Scholars have calculated that a vessel of this size would hold about forty-three thousand tons.

The rain lasted forty days and nights covering the earth with water for 150 days. Several accounts from the ancient world (other than the Scriptures) record stories of the Flood and some even recount versions of Noah's ark.

After almost a year on the water, the ark came to rest on Mount Ararat in what is now Turkey. Various attempts to locate the ark's remains have not uncovered indisputable evidence that the ark still exists. However, several archaeologists, who have braved shifting glaciers and dangerously unpredictable weather in their explorations, still claim that the ark may be caught beneath the ice.

ESCAPE FROM PHARAOH

Having been raised in an Egyptian household as the adopted grandson of the Pharaoh, Moses nevertheless was very aware of his Israelite heritage and eventually became very resentful of the slavery of his people.

One day Moses observed an Israelite slave being beaten. Moses' anger overcame him and he killed the Egyptian oppressor. This sealed his fate with Pharaoh, who would have had Moses put to death if he could have been apprehended. But Moses fled for his life. He left Egypt, headed into the Midian desert, and became a sheepherder. Forty years later, Moses returned to Egypt at God's direction to free the Israelites from slavery.

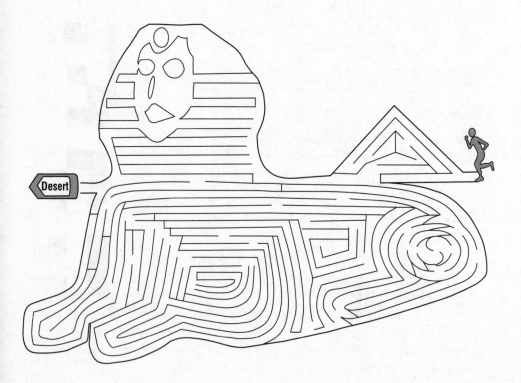

LUKE 15

Lost . . . and found. In Luke 15 Jesus tells about three things that were lost and then found. Most of the answers for this crossword come from that chapter. *Continued on following pages.*

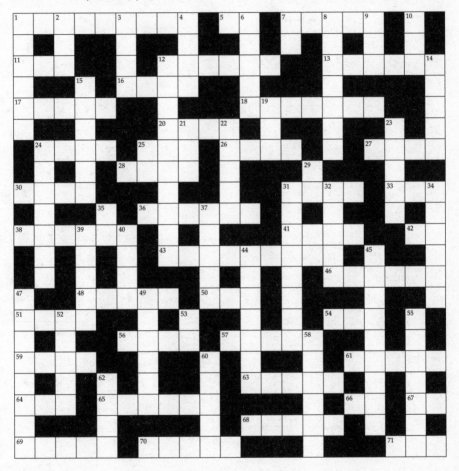

Across

1 Man's response who found his lost sheep (Luke 15:5)

5 "Your brother was dead and ___ alive again" (Luke 15:32).

7 The son who became angry (Luke 15:25)

11 Compensate

12 "I am no longer worthy to be ___ your son" (Luke 15:19).

13 The ____ and nine (Luke 15:4, KJV)

16 Nourishment

17 The brother's complaint: "I ____ transgressed your commandment; . . . yet you ____ gave me a young goat" (Luke 15:29).

18 The younger son asked for his "allotment" of his inheritance (Luke 15:12).

20 Swine food (Luke 15:16)

24 Search (Luke 15:8, KJV)

25 See (past tense) (Luke 15:20)

26 Female spouse

27 Jesus said, "A certain man had two ____" (Luke 15:11).

28 The shepherd, the woman, and the father each had something of value "disappear" (Luke 15:4, 8, 24).

30 Greater (Luke 15:7)

31 Opposite of alive (Luke 15:32)

33 At this moment (Luke 15:25)

36 The father expressed his affection to his son in this way (Luke 15:20).

38 Male parent (Luke 15:12)

41 Null and ____

42 "____ what woman" (Luke 15:8)

43 "Friends and ____" (Luke 15:6, 9)

46 Sufficient (Luke 15:17)

48 The prodigal's confession: "I have sinned against heaven and in your ____" (Luke 15:21).

50 "Distant" country (Luke 15:13)

51 The father ordered the servants to "bring out the best ____" (Luke 15:22).

54 Yours and mine

56 "He began to be in ____" (Luke 15:14).

57 Possessions (Luke 15:12)

59 Ceased living

61 When the son came home "they began to be ____" (Luke 15:24).

63 "Safe and ____" (Luke 15:27)

64 Supreme being

65 Starvation (Luke 15:17)

66 "Rejoice with ___" (Luke 15:6, 9)

67 ___ merry; ___ glad (Luke 15:24, 32)

68 A man who lost one of these searched until he found it (Luke 15:4)

69 "___ a lamp . . . and search carefully until she finds it" (Luke 15:8)

70 Discovers (Luke 15:4, 8)

71 The woman originally had ___ pieces of silver (Luke 15:8)

Down

1 To feel remorse and change your mind (Luke 15:7, 10)

2 Happiness (Luke 15:7)

3 Young cow (Luke 15:23)

4 "It was right that we should . . . be ___" (Luke 15:32)

6 Brush clean (Luke 15:8)

7 "When he has found it, he lays it ___ his shoulders, rejoicing" (Luke 15:5)

8 The son's homecoming was celebrated with "music and ___ (Luke 15:25)

9 Dashed (Luke 15:20)

10 The father's invitation to celebrate: "Let us ___ and be merry" (Luke 15:23)

12 The father's "mercy" (Luke 15:20)

14 "All #62 Down I have is ___" (Luke 15:31)

15 The ___ famine meant there was not enough food (Luke 15:14)

19 Opposite of on (Luke 15:20)

21 To be in debt

22 Pigs (Luke 15:15)

23 Valuable items that the woman lost (Luke 15:8)

24 The prodigal son's was empty (Luke 15:16)

25 "___ he divided to them his livelihood" (Luke 15:12)

29 You (old English)

31 Wasted; consumed (Luke 15:30)

32 "I will ___ and go to my father" (Luke 15:18)

34 Having value (Luke 15:19)

35 "___ came to himself" (Luke 15:17)

37 Rigid

39 The woman searched through her "dwelling" to find what was lost (Luke 15:8)

40 Jewelry to wear on a finger (Luke 15:22)

44 Prostitutes (Luke 15:30)

45 Traveled (Luke 15:13)

47 Playboy (Luke 15:13)

49 Where angels rejoice when sinners repent (Luke 15:7)

52 His father's servants had an adequate supply of this, but the son was without (Luke 15:17)

53 If she loses one coin, she searches carefully "until she finds ____?" (Luke 5:8)

55 Object lesson (Luke 15:3)

58 One who sins (Luke 15:7)

60 Employed (Luke 15:17)

62 "All ____ I have is #14 Down" (Luke 15:31)

LOADING THE BOAT

Noah was a "just man" who was righteous before God. For that reason, Noah and his family were saved from destruction when God decided to destroy all other life on dry land by a flood. God told Noah to build a large craft into which he was to gather his family and two of "every living thing of all flesh" so that the earth might be replenished when the flood waters receded (Genesis 6:19).

It is interesting to speculate whether or not this gathering of animals included fish and other sea creatures since they could have survived the flood on their own.

Help Noah with the complicated task of gathering all the animals into the ark. Do not cross over any of your paths.

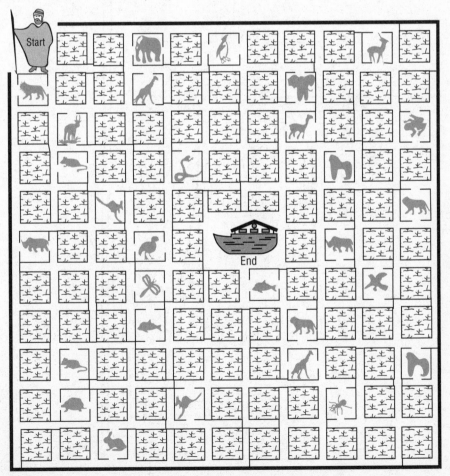

THE GOOD SHEPHERD

The symbolism of the Good Shepherd is found in both the Old and New Testaments. In Psalm 23, David asserts, "The LORD is my shepherd" (v. 1). Jesus, too, used the example of the shepherd. In a parable, he told of the shepherd with one hundred sheep and he posed a question: If the shepherd loses one sheep, will he not leave the other ninety-nine to go and search for the lost one? Jesus' care for us, his sheep, is so profound, that he is in constant search of the lost sheep among us.

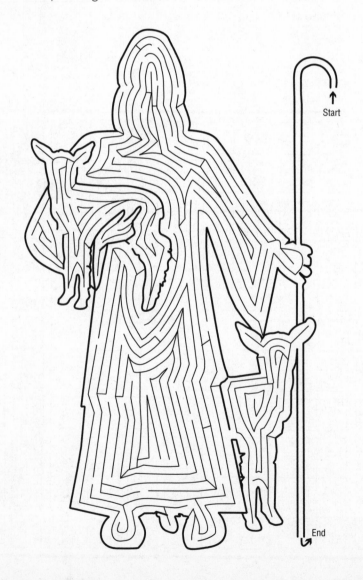

Start

End

SONG OF SOLOMON

The names of plants, birds, and animals in the Song of Solomon are the words you'll need to complete this crossword! *Continued on following pages.*

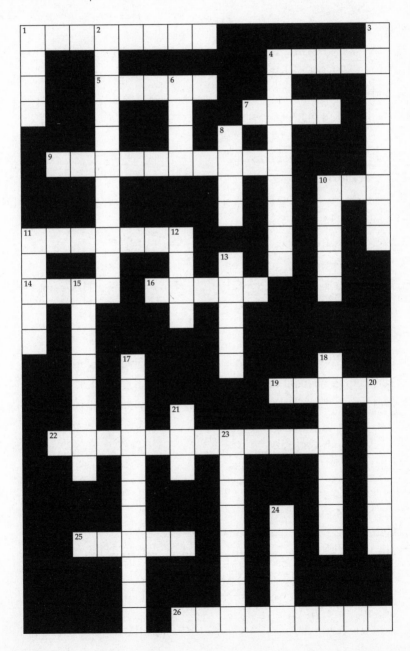

Across

1 Come with me from Lebanon . . . from the mountains of the ____ (4:8)

4 Your teeth are like a flock of shorn ____ which have come up from the washing (4:2)

5 A bundle of ____ is my beloved to me (1:13)

7 Come with me from Lebanon . . . from the ____s' dens (4:8)

9 The time of singing has come, and the voice of the ____ is heard in our land (2:12)

10 The beams of our houses are cedar, and our rafters of ____ (1:17)

11 ____ and cinnamon (4:14)

14 My ____ , my perfect one (5:2)

16 His locks are wavy, and black as a ____ (5:11)

19 Follow in the footsteps of the flock, and feed your little ____ beside the shepherds' tents (1:8)

22 With all the trees of ____ , myrrh and aloes (4:14)

25 With all the trees of frankincense, myrrh and ____ (4:14)

26 They made me the keeper of the ____ , but my own . . . I have not kept (1:6)

Down

1 Like a ____ among thorns, so is my love among the daughters (2:2)

2 Your temples behind your veil are like a piece of ____ (4:3)

3 Like an ____ among the trees of the woods, so is my beloved among the sons (2 words) (2:3)

4 ____ and saffron (4:14)

6 I am the ____ of Sharon (2:1)

8 I charge you, O daughters of Jerusalem, by the gazelles or by the ____ of the field (2:7)

10 Catch us the ____ . . . that spoil the vines (2:15)

11 The beams of our houses are ____ , and our rafters of fir (1:17)

12 My beloved is like a gazelle or a young ____ (2:9)

13 His cheeks are like a bed of spices, banks of scented ____ (5:13)

15 They made me the keeper of the vineyards, but my own ____ I have not kept (1:6)

17 My beloved is to me a cluster of ____ ____ in the vineyards of En Gedi (2 words) (1:14)

18 I charge you, O daughters of Jerusalem, by the ____ or by the does of the field, do not stir up nor awaken love until it pleases (2:7)

20 Spikenard and ____ (4:14)

21 The ____ tree puts forth her green figs (2:13)

23 Calamus and ____ (4:14)

24 I have compared you, my love, to my ____ among Pharaoh's chariots (1:9)

THE GREAT SHEPHERD

Decode one of the greatest statements in the Bible from the Great Shepherd to us, his sheep!

Clue: MESSIAH is EKGGUAL

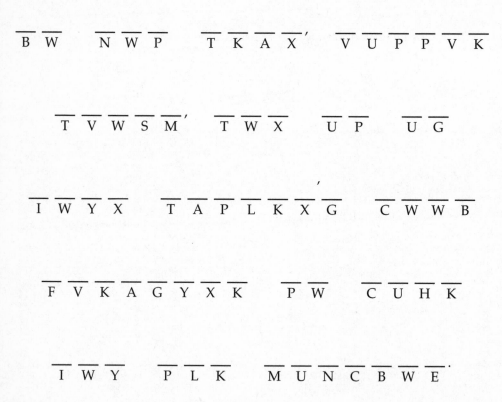

B W   N W P   T K A X '   V U P P V K

T V W S M '   T W X   U P   U G

I W Y X   T A P L K X G   C W W B

F V K A G Y X K   P W   C U H K

I W Y   P L K   M U N C B W E.

SIGNIFICANT SEVENS

Although Bible scholars do not all agree on the significance of the number seven in the Scripture, there is little doubt that it has played a frequent role in God's dealing with man. From the seven days of creation in Genesis to the seven seals in Revelation, the number occurs in nearly every book of the Bible. Some of the most memorable occurrences include the seven loaves, which at Jesus' hand fed the multitude and then filled seven baskets; the year of Jubilee which followed seven cycles of seven years; the seven times the Israelites marched around the walls of Jericho; and the seven statements of Christ from the cross.

Travel any direction to an adjacent block with the number seven from beginning to end.

↓ Start

7	6	5	3	2	5	1	6	7	7	7	9	4	9	5	0	2	7	1	4	7	7	5	9	4	0
0	7	7	7	9	7	8	7	4	2	1	7	7	7	0	7	8	7	7	5	6	1	7	7	7	6
7	9	5	0	7	0	7	0	3	3	4	8	0	1	7	7	3	2	7	0	4	3	2	0	3	7
7	6	3	1	8	2	6	7	0	4	9	6	5	2	8	6	7	5	7	7	2	7	1	9	1	7
4	7	7	4	4	7	5	7	7	0	8	6	5	7	4	6	7	9	2	8	7	7	8	0	7	3
2	1	5	7	6	7	7	0	9	7	5	7	7	9	7	0	2	7	5	4	7	9	2	7	4	2
1	5	7	3	9	8	7	4	3	2	7	1	6	8	5	7	3	7	6	7	5	2	7	3	1	6
6	7	0	4	5	8	3	8	6	2	1	7	0	2	3	7	9	1	7	7	8	5	0	7	7	7
2	8	1	7	7	7	9	7	7	5	0	1	7	9	8	7	4	9	7	3	2	0	4	7	5	0
2	1	4	7	6	0	7	8	9	7	5	8	0	8	7	4	1	7	3	7	9	5	4	7	1	4
3	7	9	3	7	5	3	1	3	7	6	3	1	9	7	5	6	5	0	8	7	2	7	9	5	0
7	7	2	2	7	4	7	5	7	6	8	4	7	7	6	7	3	1	7	7	3	4	1	7	2	0
7	4	2	7	2	4	6	7	3	5	4	7	3	8	0	7	4	7	0	4	9	5	8	7	5	2
3	3	4	7	0	0	2	7	1	5	0	7	4	9	1	7	1	7	2	8	3	6	7	7	7	7
4	0	2	5	7	6	9	7	2	4	7	8	5	8	7	0	2	4	0	7	0	7	9	2	3	9
7	7	7	7	7	3	8	5	7	7	8	4	7	7	9	2	3	1	8	0	7	3	5	7	7	4
1	2	5	0	7	4	1	3	9	5	6	2	4	9	5	7	4	2	9	7	3	8	3	0	7	9
5	7	7	4	7	7	7	7	7	8	0	1	7	8	9	7	7	4	7	0	7	7	7	2	7	0
7	6	9	0	5	8	2	8	7	5	3	7	5	7	8	2	4	7	5	3	8	5	7	9	7	3
7	5	6	7	7	7	1	7	4	7	7	2	3	9	7	7	7	3	7	2	5	1	7	7	4	0
7	7	7	7	5	9	7	5	9	0	4	6	7	7	1	2	0	5	0	7	2	7	3	9	7	7

↑ End

NO DOUBT

No doubt, this was not what anyone had in mind.

Clue: MESSIAH is TXLLDVU

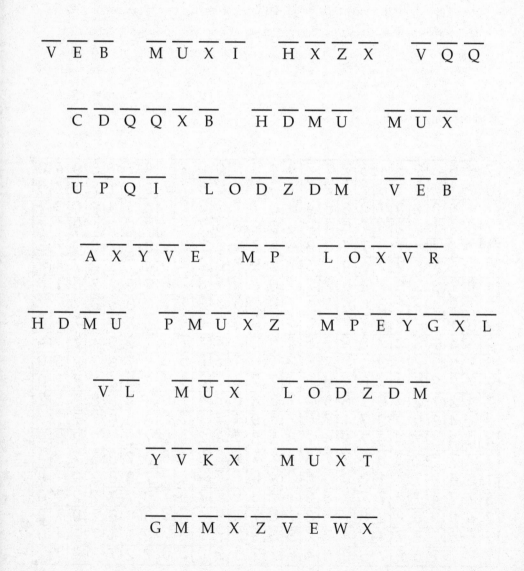

V E B   M U X I   H X Z X   V Q Q

C D Q Q X B   H D M U   M U X

U P Q I   L O D Z D M   V E B

A X Y V E   M P   L O X V R

H D M U   P M U X Z   M P E Y G X L

V L   M U X   L O D Z D M

Y V K X   M U X T

G M M X Z V E W X

YOUR DESTINY

Your destiny is awesome.

Clue: MESSIAH is QIGGMET

FYH   KI   EPP'   KMHT

YRZIMPIX   JEWI'

FITCPXMRS   EG   MR   E

QMVVCV   HTI   SPCVA   CJ

HTI   PCVX'   EVI   FIMRS

HVERGJCVQIX   MRHC   HTI

GEQI   MQESI   JVCQ

SPCVA   HC   SPCVA.

THE RETURN HOME

The life of the prodigal son that Jesus told about in a parable in Luke 15:11–32 is filled with difficult twists and turns. The young son pressured his father for his inheritance and then set out on a wild life of pleasure and excess that cost him everything he had inherited.

The young son was lost in his waywardness as his wanderings led him to the "pits" of the pig sty. There he determined to return home to become his father's sevant. But instead of servanthood, he was welcomed back by his father with a great feast as a beloved son. The older son, who had conducted his life in a much wiser manner, was angered by the celebration and confronted his father. The father declared that nothing had been taken away from the older son and everything that the father had belonged to him. What had been dead was now alive, and what was lost had been found. And so the father rejoiced.

Start ↓

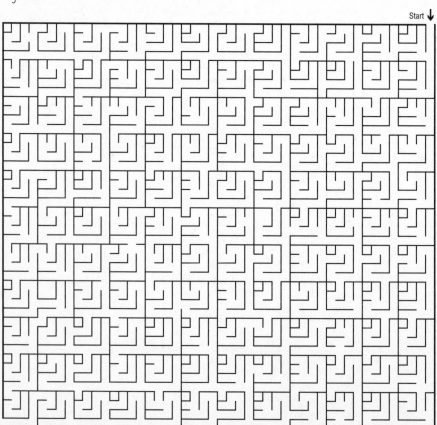

End ←

ACTIONS SPEAK LOUDER THAN WORDS

Was Jesus the first to say, "actions speak louder than words"?

Clue: MESSIAH is RPIIEOU

U P   H U Y   T Y P I   G Y X

F Y Q P   R P   T Y P I   G Y X

A P P D   R Z   H Y K T I ;   O G T

X U P   H Y K T   H U E M U   Z Y B

U P O K   E I   G Y X   R E G P

L B X   X U P   S O X U P K I '

H U Y   I P G X   R P .

1 CORINTHIANS 13

Put the missing words from 1 Corinthians 13 in the acrostic grid on the next page . . . and you'll complete an important message about the theme of this chapter. (Note: The first part of the message has been provided for you.)

Though I speak with the tongues of men and of angels, but have not love, I have become sounding brass or a clanging cymbal. And though I have the gift of prophecy, and understand all mysteries and all knowledge, and though I have all faith, so that I could remove mountains, but have not love, I am nothing. And though I bestow all my goods to feed the poor, and though I give my body to be burned, but have not love, it profits me nothing.

Love ___ long and ___ ___ ; love does ___ ___ ; love does ___
     17   15   5

___ ___ , is ___ ___ ___ ; does ___ ___ ___ , does ___ ___ ___
1   4   12   13

___ , is ___ ___ , ___ ___ ___ ; does ___ ___ ___ ___ , but rejoices
   10   9   6

in the ___ ; ___ all things, ___ all things, ___ all things, ___ all things.
   18 22   8   16   3

Love ___ ___ . But whether there are prophecies, they will fail; whether
     19

there are tongues, they will cease; whether there is knowledge, it will vanish

away. For we know in part and we prophesy in part. But when that which is

___ has come, then that which is in part will be done away.
20

When I was a child, I spoke as a child, I understood as a child, I thought as a

child; but when I ___ ___ ___ , I put away childish things. For now we see in
         11

a mirror, dimly, but then ___ ___ ___ . Now I know in part, but then I shall
         14

know just ___ ___ ___ ___ ___ .
     21

And now ___ faith, hope, love, these three; but the ___ of these is love.
    2   7

1   __ __ __ P __ __ __ __ __ __ __ __ __ __ __

2   __ __ __ __ E

3   __ __ __ R __ __

4   __ __ __ __ __ F __ __ __ __ __

5   __ __ __ E __ __ __

6   __ __ __ __ __ __ __ C __ __ __ __ __ __ __ __ __ __

7   __ __ __ __ T __ __ __

8   __ __ L __ __ __ __ __

9   __ __ __ __ __ __ __ O __ __ __ __

10   __ __ __ __ __ __ V __ __ __ __

THERE IS NO FEAR IN LOVE, BUT . . .

11   __ __ C __ __ __ __ __ __ __

12   __ __ __ __ __ __ A __ __ __ __ __ __ __ __

13   __ __ __ S __ __ __ __ __ __ __ __

14   __ __ __ __ T __ __ __ __ __

15   __ S __ __ __ __

16   __ O __ __ __

17   __ U __ __ __ __ __

18   T __ __ __ __

19   __ __ __ __ __ F __ __ __ __

20   __ E __ __ __ __ __

21   __ __ __ A __ __ __ __ __ __ __ __ __

22   __ __ __ R __

UNSCRAMBLE PHARAOH

Pharaoh's refusal to allow the children of Israel to return to the promised land led to great misery for the Egyptian people. Below is a list of the ten plagues that fell on the Egyptians as a result of Pharaoh's stubbornness. After unscrambling the words, unscramble the circled letters to find out why Pharaoh refused to let the Israelites go.

LODOB   _ _ _ _ Ⓞ

GORFS   _ Ⓞ _ _ _

CILE   _ _ _ Ⓞ

LIFES   _ _ _ Ⓞ _

LICENSEPET   _ Ⓞ _ _ _ _ Ⓞ _ _

SOLIB   _ _ _ _ _

LAHI   Ⓞ Ⓞ _ _

CUTLOSS   _ _ _ _ _ Ⓞ _

DRSNAKES   _ Ⓞ Ⓞ _ _ _ _ _

HATED   Ⓞ _ _ _ Ⓞ

Scrambled letters:

_ _ _ _ _ _ _ _ _ _ _ _ _

Unscrambled letters:

_ _ _ _ _ _ _ _ _ _ _ _ _

Scripture Pool
EXODUS 7:17; 8:2, 16, 21; 9:3, 9, 18; 10:4, 21; 11:5

REVELATION QUIZ

Revelation is a book in which numbers abound—frequently as symbols. Using the numbers indicated by the clues, work the equation to come up with the "perfect" answer. All the numbers are found in the book of Revelation. You may need your calculator for this one!

Number of Jews receiving the seal of the living God
(Revelation 7:4)   = _____

Divided by . . .
Number equal to ten percent of the army of the horsemen
(Revelation 9:16)   ÷ _____

Multiplied by . . .
Number of men killed in the earthquake after the murdered
prophets ascended (Revelation 11:13)   × _____

Minus . . .
Number of living creatures (full of eyes) surrounding the throne
(Revelation 4:6)   − _____

Divided by . . .
Number of edges on the sword coming from the Son of man's
mouth (Revelation 1:16)   ÷ _____

Multiplied by . . .
Number of months locusts were allowed to sting
(Revelation 9:5)   × _____

Plus . . .
Number of thrones around God's throne (Revelation 4:4)   + _____

Divided by . . .
Number of lampstands (Revelation 2:1)   ÷ _____

Plus . . .
Number of pearls used for each gate in the New Jerusalem
(Revelation 21:21)   + _____

Divided by . . .
Number of gates on each wall of New Jerusalem
(Revelation 21:13)   ÷ _____

Number of churches that received the Revelation from John
(Revelation 1:4)   = _____

THE OPEN WORD

The Bible is the most widely read book in the world. It continues to appear on the list of best-selling books every year. Yet owning a Bible does not assure its owner of a relationship with God.

The book of John says, "In the beginning was the Word, and the Word was with God, and the Word was God. . . . And the Word became flesh and dwelt among us, and we beheld His glory, the glory as of the only begotten of the Father, full of grace and truth" (v. 1, 14).

The Word of God is not just a beautiful piece of literature or an historical account of our spiritual roots; it is literally the Word of God to us and our path to him through Jesus Christ his Son.

Start at "In the beginning" and finish at "Amen."

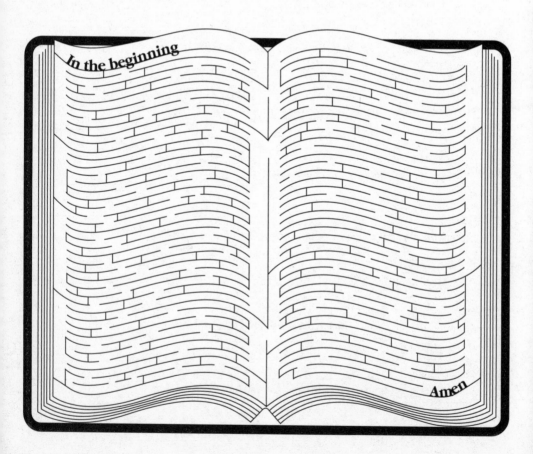

ALPHA AND OMEGA

Start →

←End

Alpha is the first letter of the Greek alphabet, Omega the last letter.

Three times in the book of Revelation, the phrase is used. The first time, in Revelation 1:8, God the Father spoke: "I am the Alpha and the Omega, the Beginning and the End . . . who is and who was and who is to come, the Almighty."

In Revelation 21:6 and 22:13, Jesus was the one speaking: "I am the Alpha and the Omega, the Beginning and the End" and, "I am the Alpha and Omega, the Beginning and the End, the First and the Last."

The threefold use of the phrase underscores its importance.

The phrase points to Christ as being both the source and the sum of everything—the Creator and the Culminator.

THE SIXTH SEAL

Complete the message below to discover what is said in the wake of the opening of the sixth seal, and its resulting great earthquake, in the book of Revelation.

Clue: MESSIAH is AIUUEMF

> The kings of the earth, the great men, the rich men, the commanders, the mighty men, every slave and every free man, hid themselves in the caves and in the rocks of the mountains, and said to the mountains and rocks,

"

H M B B   Y Z   S U   M Z J

F E J I   S U   H V Y A   T F I

H M K I   Y H   F E A   Q F Y

U E T U   Y Z   T F I   T F V Y Z I

M Z J   H V Y A   T F I   Q V M T F

Y H   T F I   B M A L !   H Y V

T F I   G V I M T   J M O   Y H

F E U   Q V M T F   F M U   K Y A I '

M Z J   Q F Y   E U   M L B I   T Y

U T M Z J ?"

PSALM 23

One of the most beloved and frequently memorized psalms is Psalm 23. See how many of the words you can supply for the grid below without looking up this passage in the Bible.

The LORD is my shepherd; I shall not want. He (3) me to (25) (19) in (6) (12); He leads me beside the (20) (29). He (9) my soul; He (7) me in the (1) of (2) for (16) (23) sake.

Yea, (22) I (4) through the (30) of the (5) of (17), I will fear no (24); for You are (8) me; Your (27) and Your (28), they (10) me.

You (15) a (32) before me in the presence of my (14); You (26) my head with oil; My cup (18) over. (21) (31) and (11) shall follow me all the days of my life; and I will dwell in the (13) of the LORD forever.

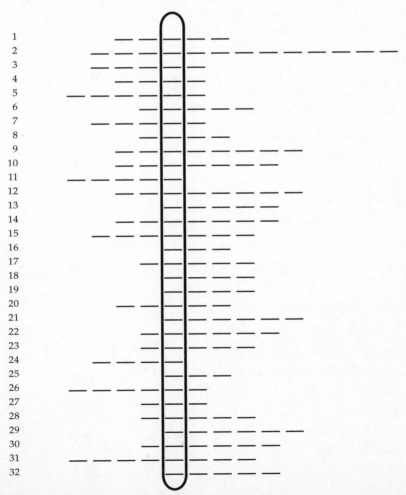

WATER INTO WINE

When Jesus turned the water into wine he made enough so the wedding host wouldn't run out again. Complete the puzzle below to find out how much water miraculously became wine.

The number of baths of oil given to the woodsmen who cut timber for the temple (2 Chronicles 2:10)
$=$ _____

Minus . . .
The capacity in baths of the Sea of the temple (1 Kings 7:26)
$-$ _____

Divided by . . .
The number of measures of wheat owed by the debtor after his bill was reduced by the unjust steward (Luke 16:7)
$\div$ _____

Multiplied by . . .
The number of homers of barley Hosea paid to get Gomer back (Hosea 3:2)
$\times$ _____

Multiplied by . . .
The fraction of an ephah of fine flour offered with a young bull as a sacriftce (Numbers 15:9)
$\times$ _____

Minus . . .
The fraction of a hin of wine that was to be offered daily as a drink offering (Exodus 29:40)
$-$ _____

Divided by . . .
The least amount of homers of quail gathered in the desert when God sent flocks of quail to eat (Numbers 11:32)
$\div$ _____

Minus . . .
The omer is _____ of an ephah (Exodus 16:36)
$-$ _____

Plus . . .
The number of omers of manna gathered for each person on the sixth day of the week (Exodus 16:22)
$+$ _____

Divided by . . .
The number of seahs of barley sold for a shekel during the famine in Samaria (2 Kings 7:1)
$\div$ _____

Equals . . .
The number of waterpots filled with water that Jesus turned into wine (John 2:6)
$=$ _____

ANSWERS TO BRAIN BUILDERS

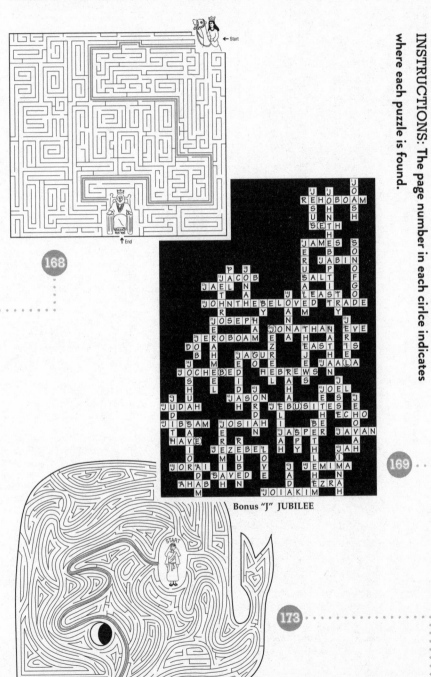

168

169

173

Bonus "J" JUBILEE

INSTRUCTIONS: The page number in each cirlce indicates where each puzzle is found.

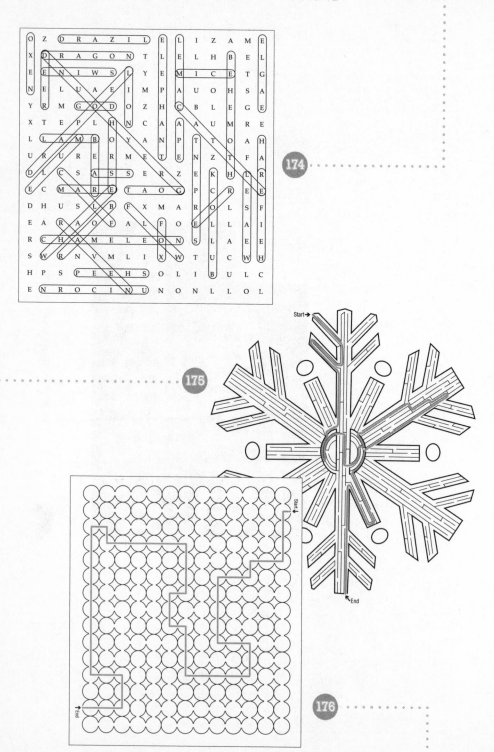

174

175

176

$$7 \times 2 \times 2 \times 17 + 150 - 40 + 10 + 3 + 4 - 3 = 600 \quad \textbf{177}$$

178

And God blessed them, and God said unto them, Be fruitful and multiply, and replenish the earth, and subdue it: and have dominion over the fish of the sea, and over the fowl of the air, and over every living thing that moveth upon the earth. (Genesis 1:28)

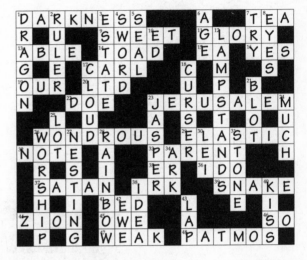

179

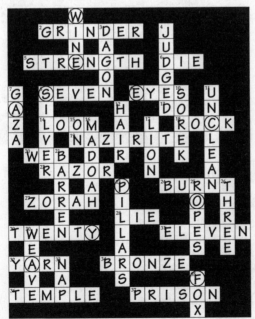

Unscrambled letters:
WAY OF ESCAPE

181

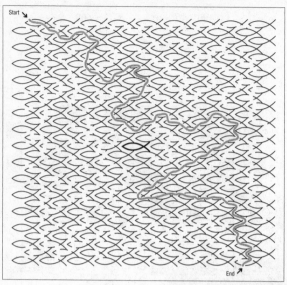

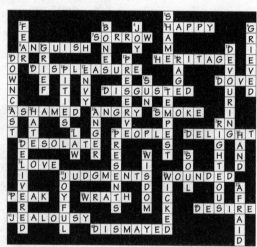

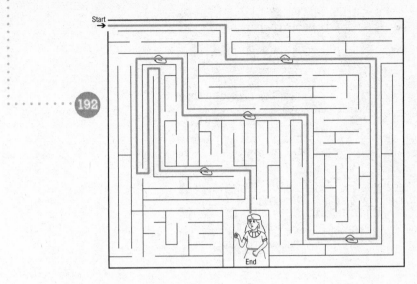

192

193

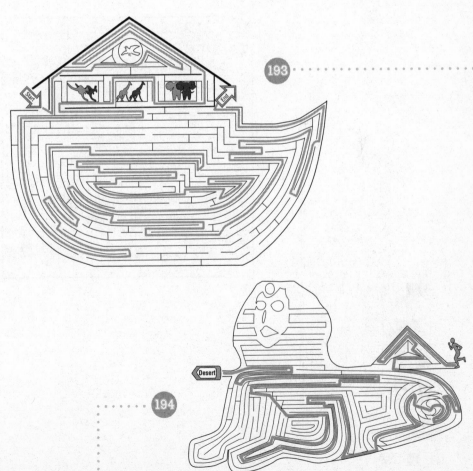

194

195

199

200

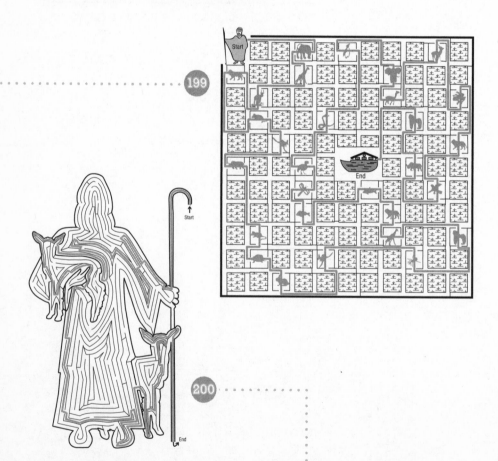

Do not fear, little flock, for it is your Father's good pleasure to give you the kingdom. (Luke 12:32)

201

205

And they were all filled with the Holy Spirit and began to speak with other tongues, as the Spirit gave them utterance. (Acts 2:4, NKJ)

206

But we all, with unveiled face, beholding as in a mirror the glory of the Lord, are being transformed into the same image from glory to glory. (2 Corinthians 3:18)

207

208

209 He who does not love Me does not keep My words; and the word which you hear is not Mine but the Father's who sent Me. (John 14:24)

210

NOT **P**ARADE ITSELF
ABID**E**
ENDU**R**ES
NOT PU**F**FED UP
NOT **E**NVY
NOT REJOI**C**E IN INIQUITY
GREA**T**EST
BE**L**IEVES
THINKS N**O** EVIL
NOT PRO**V**OKED
THERE IS NO **F**EAR IN LOVE. BUT…
BE**C**AME A MAN
NOT BEH**A**VE RUDELY
NOT **S**EEK ITS OWN
FACE **T**O FACE
IS KIND
H**O**PES
S**U**FFERS
TRUTH
NEVER **F**AILS
P**E**RFECT
AS I **A**LSO AM KNOWN
BEA**R**S

There is no fear in love; but perfect love casts out fear. (1 John 4:18)

212
Blood	Pestilence	Locusts
Frogs	Boils	Darkness
Lice	Hail	Death
Flies		

Unscrambled letters: HARDENED HEART

$$144{,}000 \div 20{,}000{,}000 \times 7{,}000 - 4 \div 2 \times 5 + 24 \div 7 + 1 \div 3 = 7$$

213

214

In the beginning

Amen

Start →

215

← End

$20,000 - 2,000 \div 80 \times 1.5 \times .3 - .25 \div 10 - .1 + 2 \div 2 = 6$

218

Fall on us and
hide us from
the face of
Him who sits
on the throne
and from the
wrath of the
Lamb! For
the great day
of His wrath
has come,
and who is
able to stand?
(Revelation
6:16–17)

216

PATHS
RIGHTEOUSNESS
MAKES
WALK
SHADOW
GREEN
LEADS
WITH
RESTORES
COMFORT
MERCY
PASTURES
HOUSE
ENEMIES
PREPARE
HIS
DEATH
RUNS
DOWN
STILL
SURELY
THOUGH
NAMES
EVIL
LIE
ANOINT
ROD
STAFF
WATERS
VALLEY
GOODNESS
TABLE

217

THE LORD IS MY SHEPHERD, I SHALL NOT WANT